MUSKOKA RESORTS

THEN *and* NOW

Andrew Hind *and* Maria Da Silva

DUNDURN
NATURAL HERITAGE
TORONTO

Editor: Allison Hirst
Design: Jennifer Scott
Printer: Marquis

Library and Archives Canada Cataloguing in Publication

Hind, Andrew
    Muskoka resorts : then and now / Andrew Hind and Maria Da Silva.

Includes bibliographical references and index.
Issued also in electronic format.
ISBN 978-1-55488-857-3

1. Resorts--Ontario--Muskoka (District municipality)--History. 2. Historic hotels--Ontario--Muskoka (District municipality)--History. I. Da Silva, Maria II. Title.

FC3095.M88H56 2011   971.3'16   C2011-900939-0

1   2   3   4   5   15   14   13   12   11

We acknowledge the support of the **Canada Council for the Arts** and the **Ontario Arts Council** for our publishing program. We also acknowledge the financial support of the **Government of Canada** through the **Canada Book Fund** and **Livres Canada Books**, and the **Government of Ontario** through the **Ontario Book Publishers Tax Credit** program, and the **Ontario Media Development Corporation**.

Care has been taken to trace the ownership of copyright material used in this book. The author and the publisher welcome any information enabling them to rectify any references or credits in subsequent editions.

J. Kirk Howard, President

Printed and bound in Canada.
www.dundurn.com

Front cover images: (top) Aerial view of Windermere House, *courtesy of Windermere House*; (bottom) Deerhurst Resort, circa 1900s, *courtesy of Deerhurst Resort.*

Dundurn	Gazelle Book Services Limited	Dundurn
3 Church Street, Suite 500	White Cross Mills	2250 Military Road
Toronto, Ontario, Canada	High Town, Lancaster, England	Tonawanda, NY
M5E 1M2	LA1 4XS	U.S.A. 14150

This book is dedicated to the entrepreneurs and visionaries of yesteryear who established Muskoka's inns, and to the current owners of these historic resorts who keep the tradition of hospitality alive for future generations

CONTENTS

FOREWORD

When Andrew and Maria asked me to write this foreword about this superb and expansive story about the Muskoka Resorts, I said yes because it is a subject that has special appeal to so many folks who, like myself, have come to love Muskoka.

I found these stories of hope, hard work, memories, failure, and success brought to life 150 years of history that helped shape Muskoka into this special and unique place it is.

And though Muskoka has changed dramatically from its hard and challenging logging and farming base, it didn't take long for its special geography of water, rock, and forest to shape the final destiny for the district.

This book will help preserve and strengthen the special feeling many of us share. Muskoka has a unique place in our hearts and keeps drawing us back.

KEN FOWLER

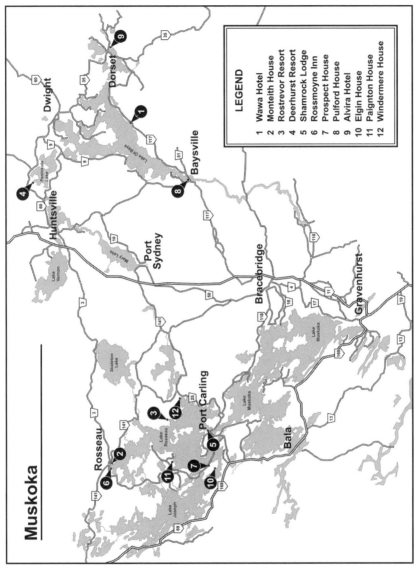

Muskoka

LEGEND

1 Wawa Hotel
2 Monteith House
3 Rostrevor Resort
4 Deerhurst Resort
5 Shamrock Lodge
6 Rossmoyne Inn
7 Prospect House
8 Pulford House
9 Alvira Hotel
10 Elgin House
11 Paignton House
12 Windermere House

The Muskoka Region,
Ontario, Canada.

Map by James Hind.

PREFACE

Try to imagine Muskoka without Windermere House's white towers rising over Lake Rosseau or without the name Deerhurst to instantly conjure up images of refined hospitality. Muskoka's resorts are regional icons, symbols of its status as a beloved tourist destination and a summer playground for vacationers.

It's been that way for more than a century. Long before there were private cottages, a wide range of resorts — some large and luxurious, others little more than family homes that had been opened up to tourists — lured people to this beautiful country, offering warm hospitality and an escape from the stresses that, even then, were associated with city life.

In a very real sense, the modern Muskoka we know and love was built on the foundations established by these early hotels. True, settlers and logging companies opened up the region to habitation, but it was the tourist industry that allowed Muskoka to sustain itself once the land had proven beyond cultivation and the forests had been cleared of harvestable timber. It's therefore fitting that timeless resorts such as Deerhurst, Windermere House, and Clevelands House should define Muskoka; some would argue Muskoka should rightfully be called "Resort Country" rather than "Cottage Country."

Few people realize the sheer number of summer hotels that once existed here. Today they are a disappearing breed; most have vanished altogether, and many that remain are being converted to fractional cottage properties, which will forever change their character and appearance. A century ago, however, there were well over a hundred resorts active in Muskoka, each with its own unique charm and personality, each with its own stories to tell.

The purpose of *Muskoka Resorts: Then and Now* is to preserve the history and memories of some of these summer hotels. While most readers will be familiar with Windermere House or Deerhurst, by reputation if nothing else, how many have heard of the Alvira Hotel or the Rossmoyne Inn? Probably not many, but that doesn't make their stories any less worthy of preservation. In fact, one could argue — as we did — that because the number of people who remember these resorts are dwindling as time inevitably marches on, it becomes vitally important to record their memories and help commit the history of these old hotels to paper. In such a way, those memories will live on. By design, therefore, the resorts selected for inclusion in this book represent a broad cross-section of those that have existed in Muskoka over the years: the large and the small, the opulent and the rustic, some long gone and some that are still with us. We included hotels from the geographic breadth and width of the region. You'll not only discover the histories of twelve beloved resorts, but also gain an understanding of how the tourist industry shaped every corner of Muskoka.

While conducting our research, we had the opportunity to visit several of the region's hotels to experience first-hand their own particular magic. We gazed out onto the shimmering waters of Lake Rosseau from our room at the Rosseau Resort, just as people a century ago surely would have done when historic Paignton House stood on the same site. We thrilled at the musical talents on display during the stage show that has made Deerhurst Resort famous, and enjoyed learning that *this* was the very stage where a young Shania Twain got her start in the music industry. And we marvelled at the timeless charm of Windermere House, so serene that you feel as if you have been transported back in time. Priceless memories were made, which brought us closer to the subject-matter and made this book highly personal.

Muskoka Resorts: Then and Now is a celebration of the summer resorts that came to define this region, and created countless cherished memories for so many people over the years … us included.

Preface

• • • • • • • • • • • • • • • •

Muskoka Resorts: Then and Now devotes a full chapter to twelve of the region's resorts, allowing their stories to be told in depth. In most cases, the detail we lavished upon each entry is greater than that which you'll find in any other single source. That was our intent; rather than casting our net wide and doing none of the resorts justice, we focused our efforts on just a few, with the aim of truly bringing their histories to life.

We spend a great deal of time relating the stories of the resorts' various owners, as we felt that the character of a resort is very much a reflection of the proprietor. And because resorts in those days were run by people rather than corporate entities, as many are today, learning about the owners' lives — their trials and triumphs, loss and levity — is central to understanding the development of their hotels.

Scattered throughout the text are dozens of photos, some modern but most contemporary, intended to bring the resorts to life and to serve as points of reference. Many of these photos have been donated by descendants of prior owners or by guests who visited the hotels many years ago, and, as a result, have never been published.

We firmly believe that the best way to appreciate history is to experience it first hand. To that end, each chapter includes a "See for Yourself" section that will help readers discover these resorts for themselves. In the case of hotels that are still thriving, the focus is on pointing out the historic elements that are so easily overshadowed by modern amenities and activities. When it came to the long-lost resorts, we identify the location, point out any remnants that might be found, and mention local museums that have exhibits or artifacts devoted to them. Sadly, we'll never be able to experience the thrill of walking through the front doors of these lost hotels, to discover for ourselves their charm and meet their colourful owners, but hopefully we have provided readers with the next best thing.

Because there were so many fascinating resorts to choose from for inclusion in the book, we struggled to narrow the number down to just twelve. Some others captured our imaginations so thoroughly

MUSKOKA RESORTS

that we couldn't bear to completely let them go, and so we elected
to include these — ten in total — in capsule form in the last chapter,
foreshadowing the intended sequel to this volume. Even in brief, their
stories are fascinating.

Every decision that went into designing *Muskoka Resorts: Then and
Now* was made with the goal of capturing the spirit of the twelve hotels
detailed within, and offering a glimpse into their evolution, from the
1860s until today. It's an account of enterprising owners, affluent guests,
tireless staff ... and of leisurely summer days. We hope that reading this
book will serve as an enjoyable and nostalgic journey. Writing it certainly was for us!

INTRODUCTION

BEGINNINGS

The story of Muskoka's resorts must begin with the settlement of the region, for the two go hand-in-hand. Prior to the mid-nineteenth century, Muskoka was uninhabited wilderness, a vast and rugged region consisting of endless miles of forest dotted with thousands of lakes and swamps. Its foundations, rooted in the grey granite of the Canadian Shield, erupted from beneath the earth in every direction. This made for stunningly beautiful terrain, but it also made the region imposing to prospective settlers: the dense forests were dark and foreboding, much of the land was beyond cultivation, and the harshness of the landscape obstructed transportation and communication. Muskoka was untamed, and with good reason.

Things began to change in 1868, when, in an effort to encourage more settlement, Ontario passed the Free Grants and Homesteads Act. Under this plan, the government built a network of colonization roads into the wild hinterlands of the province, and then offered one hundred acres of land to any settler who was prepared to move into these unin-habited areas (heads of families had the right to claim two hundred acres). The only stipulation was that the settler was expected to clear fifteen of those acres, build a house, and live the site continuously for at least five years. Thousands took up the offer during the following decades, founding farms and villages throughout Muskoka that gradually brought a sense of civilization to the region.

These homesteads and hamlets were established with a sense of buoyant optimism, the settlers certain that a bright future was ahead of them. As it turned out, however, the Free Grants and Homesteads Act wasn't such a great offer. Settlers soon came to realize that the only thing holding the soil together in much of Muskoka were the roots of the trees. Once the trees were felled to make room for farm fields, the thin layer of soil covering the Canadian Shield washed away. Most farms, even in the best of years, barely provided enough to sustain the farmer and his family. Prosperity through tilling the soil and cultivating crops proved elusive.

Naturally, many people were disappointed with the lack of productivity from their land and began to search for other means of making a living. They found that they could reap greater success by opening their homes to hunters and fishermen, mostly wealthy and well-born men from America, who were seeking the adventure of the Canadian wilderness. As word spread that Muskoka represented a sportsman's dream, residents found that more and more travellers began knocking on their doors, asking for a warm bed, a hearty meal, and perhaps a local guide — and they were willing to pay well for these services. The Muskoka tourist industry was born.

THE FIRST HOTELS AND THE RISE
OF THE TOURIST INDUSTRY

It wasn't long before these hunters and anglers, marvelling at the clean air, beautiful waters, and the splendour of the natural environs, began bringing their families with them. As demand for food and lodgings grew, the homes that had been converted into boarding houses were adapted to serve as hotels.

The first wilderness resort, the one that formed the template after which all those to come were modelled, was Rosseau House, or Pratt's

Hotel. In 1870, local steamship magnate Alexander P. Cockburn, eager to boost passenger traffic on his vessels, encouraged wealthy New Yorker William H. Pratt to build a luxury hotel in the village of Rosseau. It was a bold gamble. Would enough people be willing to make the long journey to Muskoka? Was the growing interest in wilderness vacations just a fad or was it here to stay? That remained to be seen.

If Pratt had any doubts, however, they were quickly dispelled by the masses of affluent tourists that flocked to his hotel almost as soon as it was opened. The demand was so great that he was compelled to expand, adding wings that more than doubled the number of guests that could be accommodated. Residents across Muskoka began to take note of Pratt's success, and in the years that followed, dozens of other hotels emerged to challenge Rosseau House.

The rise of Muskoka as a tourist destination was linked to developments that were dramatically altering people's lifestyles. Throughout the nineteenth century, the cities of the American East Coast (and Toronto, as well) underwent rapid industrialization that led to increased congestion, smoke, and heat that made them barely habitable during the summer months. The poor naturally had no escape from such inhospitable conditions, but the wealthy and the emerging middle classes could afford to flee the city for someplace more pleasant. Many were advised to do so by their physicians: "Neuroasthenia" was a catch-all diagnosis for ailments of the nervous system associated with stress and overwork, for which the prescribed cure was a holiday "in nature's embrace," physical activity in clean air, and no mental strain. Muskoka, with its refreshing waters, beautiful forests, relaxed atmosphere, and fresh, pollution-free air, fit the bill perfectly. Indeed, the air was said to be so pure as to have curative properties, rejuvenating the sick and curing those who suffered from hay fever or even far more serious ailments, such as tuberculosis (TB). In fact, the first sanatorium for TB patients in Canada was built in Gravenhurst in the late 1800s.

Muskoka's popularity was also certainly bolstered by the rave reviews that the wilderness was receiving from writers of the time: "If ever there was an Eden, we think, we must find it here," wrote George Munro Grant in *Picturesque Canada*, published in 1882. He continued:

Seldom has our eye lit upon a lovelier scene, and never, to our mind, has Nature made a more effective use of her materials. Sky, and land, and water, here all combine — as we have often seen — to make a perfect picture, the effect of which, particularly when the woods are ablaze with the colouring of a Canadian autumn, is almost indescribable.[1]

Who wouldn't be swayed by such glowing praise? Certainly countless wealthy American vacationers were, making the region the summer destination of choice for many.

THE GOLDEN ERA

By the 1890s, Muskoka had become one of the most popular holiday regions in North America, and dozens of resorts sprang up along the lakeshores of this charismatic region. Most of the more enduring and famous of Muskoka's grand hotels were established in this golden era: Deerhurst, Clevelands House, Windermere House, the Royal Muskoka Hotel, the Wawa Hotel, and Beaumaris were all up and running during this period, offering luxury accommodations in the midst of the Canadian wilderness, owners and staff working tirelessly to provide the best in hospitality and to ensure that fond memories were made. They knew that a favourable impression would result in guests returning year-after-year, perhaps for generations.

But, of course, for every Royal Muskoka and Windermere House, there were two or three smaller hotels, most of which are forgotten today. Douglas Johnston, whose grandfather operated Shamrock Lodge and who spent a summer working at a small resort during his teenage years, recalls those days:

The Muskoka Lakes were dotted with many, many family-owned smaller lodges that accommodated from

20

several families to perhaps a dozen guests. Traditionally, the same family clientele came back year after year to these smaller resorts…. The guests were not only favourably impressed by the wonder and mystique of Muskoka, but also by the character and ambience of the various resorts. Each resort had [its] own culture, with management and staff carefully catering [to] the egos and every need of the guests so that their holiday was not only a great rest, but also one not to be forgotten. The tourist folk were eager to find resorts that matched their holiday desires, offered a good respite from the cares of their work-a-day life in their home cities, and, above all, served delicious home baking and home-cooked meals.[2]

Though there was a brief hiccup during the First World War, the Golden Era of Muskoka's resorts endured into the 1920s and through the Big Band Era. At the time, the biggest names in music could be found playing in resort dance halls and ballrooms throughout the region: the Dorsey Brothers, the legendary Duke Ellington, and other giants of the industry. It was a heady time, characterized by a relentless pursuit of pleasure, and the wealthy from all over North America flocked to Muskoka each summer to indulge themselves in luxury, dancing, sport, and socializing with their peers. Indeed, the 1920s represented the apogee of the resort era, and was fittingly marked by the arrival on the scene of the grandest, most opulent of them all: Bigwin Inn, on Lake of Bays.

GETTING THERE

The journey by train and steamer was considered part of the adventure of vacationing in Muskoka, a beloved tradition that allowed expectations to slowly boil over the course of a day en route. Perhaps subconsciously, travellers also realized that without the railroads and steamships making

Muskoka accessible, there would be no resorts at which to while away carefree summer days.

Much of the credit for opening up Muskoka to tourists should go to A.P. Cockburn. Trains only went as far as Gravenhurst prior to 1886, when service was extended to Bracebridge and then Huntsville. From here, though, to reach any point in Muskoka, a person had to walk, take a stage over primitive, rutted roads, or travel by water. The latter was easiest and cheapest, and certainly the only one that wealthy tourists would willingly agree to undertake.

Cockburn visited the area in 1865 and saw the possibility of opening up the district via water navigation on the chain of lakes comprising Lake Muskoka, Lake Rosseau, and Lake Joseph. He told government officials that he would put a steamship on the lakes if they in turn would build a lock to bypass the rapids at Port Carling. The government, recognizing the value of the proposal, readily agreed. In 1866, Cockburn launched the first steamboat, the *Wenonah*, and by the time the locks were completed five years later, he had three more vessels in his growing fleet. Thanks to Cockburn's vision, Muskoka was truly accessible for the first time, allowing thousands of tourists to enjoy the hospitality of its many hotels each summer.

Regardless of where these tourists originally came from — whether it was New York, Pittsburgh, Philadelphia, or Toronto — their journey north began at Union Station in Toronto. For Americans, this brief chance to stretch their legs as they changed trains represented the halfway point of the journey. When the whistle sounded departure, travellers settled into their seats for the six-hour trip. Some were lulled to sleep by the rhythmic sound and sway of the railcar, and by the mile upon mile of rolling farmland racing past the windows. Some chatted amiably with fellow travellers, inquiring about where they were from and to which resort they were headed, perhaps even renewing acquaintances from past years. Others, generally the children, were simply too excited and could barely remain seated for the duration. But regardless of how one passed the hours, none could ignore the energy that buzzed in the cars.

Vacationers would disembark at Muskoka Wharf in Gravenhurst or Huntsville Station on Hunter's Bay, where a majestic white steamship awaited their arrival. Passengers lingered on the wharf for a time, gazing out on sun-dappled Lake Muskoka, while their trunks were stowed below decks. Then the ship's purser would usher them aboard, some to seats inside, but if the weather was fine, most elected to find a spot alongside the railing, where they could view the shoreline as they sailed past. Then the whistle would sound and the ship would slowly pull away from the dock.

A light snack and a cup of tea would be served during the course of the journey, which could be measured in minutes or hours, depending on which destination one was headed to. It didn't seem to matter how long the trip, though, as everyone enjoyed their time aboard: the sound of the ship's shrill whistle, the sight of smoke coiling up from the stack, the feeling of the engines thrumming underfoot — it was all part of an exciting experience that many never forgot. In fact, steamer trips became so popular that they became recreational attractions in their own right, with special excursions and moonlight cruises being advertised for guests of area resorts.

Douglas Johnston has fond memories of these steamships from his youth in the 1930s:

> The whistles blew piercingly as passengers disembarked at Port Carling to catch a steamer like the *Ahmic* or *Islander* that was capable of landing in shallower waters. As young boys, we were ready to carry luggage from one boat to the other to earn pin money. In the quiet moments of reflection, I can still hear the ships' pursers calling out the ports of call. Their voices were shrill but distinctive as they called out "Windermere, Wigwasson, Monteith House, Rostrevor, Stanley House, The Royal …"[3]

Like the resorts they served, most of the steamships are long gone from Muskoka's lakes — most, but not all. The piercing whistles warmly remembered by Douglas Johnson and so many others of his era can still be heard to this day, produced by Muskoka's last two remaining steam-ships, RMS *Segwun* and RMS *Wenonah II*, which collectively form what is arguably the region's premier tourist attraction. In what is a beautifully nostalgic idea, a couple of times each year these ships team with a historic resort to provide an experience very much like that which guests of bygone days would have experienced: a steamship takes you from Muskoka Wharf in Gravenhurst to the participating resort, where you enjoy overnight accommodations before the ship picks you up again the following day for the return voyage. It's not hard to imagine that such packages would be extremely popular.

DECLINE — AND RENEWAL

The stock market crash of 1929 and the Great Depression that followed forever changed the face of Muskoka tourism. Those were difficult times for the resorts. Many people no longer had the disposable income to spend on a summer vacation — luxuries, which vacations surely constitute, are the first thing to be discarded when times get tough. As a result, many resorts were forced to close off floors, wings, or lodges as the number of guests dwindled. Bats, mice, and rot moved in. More than a decade of neglect meant that once guests began to return to these facilities, they were no longer useable, and many had to be demolished or rebuilt.

These were the lucky ones. For every resort that weathered the Depression, there were two that were forced to shut down completely and were fated never to reopen. Typically, these were the smaller hotels, but their demise was no less of a loss; the closeness between proprietor and guest meant that these more intimate resorts were oftentimes the most beloved, and therefore the most dearly missed. Sadly, a great many of these resorts are forgotten today, and those that are still recalled garner only a line or two when mentioned at all.

Muskoka's resorts had great hopes that crowds would return after the Second World War: the Depression was a thing of the past, people were filled with dreams and had the money to make them a reality, and with advances in automobiles, Muskoka was closer than ever. Unfortunately, things didn't quite work out as envisioned. With air transportation now affordable, people began to shun Muskoka and other traditional destinations, instead heading off to Europe, the Caribbean, and other exotic locales. Those who did not turn their backs on Muskoka — and there were many who didn't — more often than not opted to purchase a cottage of their own rather than spend weeks on end at a hotel. Combined, these two factors delivered a near-fatal blow to area resorts.

As travel tastes were evolving, the extravagance that marked most of the largest and most famous resorts in the early decades of the century fell out of style. Some resorts were able to adapt, but others couldn't. Bigwin Inn, once the playground of royalty, millionaires, and Hollywood stars, a property widely acclaimed as the finest resort hotel in the British Empire, was one that couldn't. People were shocked when it closed its doors, but size and opulence were not enough to save a resort if it couldn't be modified quickly to conform to modern tastes. Fewer and fewer people came, so that at one point there were actually more staff than guests. Such an absurd situation clearly couldn't continue, forcing the owners to take the painful step of closing the once-grand hotel in the mid-1960s. Its demise was a warning to other resort owners: adapt or go under.

While many resorts closed during the Depression, others failed due to the inability of their owners to keep up with the public's changing moods or fell into ruin from neglect. "People didn't put money into the resorts. They just built resorts, and never put any money into them and allowed it bleed away," bemoans Archie Pain, a third-generation member of the Pain family of Paignton House.[4] In some cases, the owners simply didn't see the value of investing in resorts that were only open a few months of the year; other times they simply lacked the resources to properly maintain the aging buildings.

But of all the ways in which Muskoka's resorts met their demise, the most dramatic was as a result of the destructive power of fire. Muskoka's old resorts were many things — charming, beautiful, atmospheric — but built to last they were not. Constructed of wood, with little thought given to fireproofing or fire prevention, and often with newsprint stuffed between the walls to serve as insulation, they were Roman candles that simply needed a spark to ignite them. Unfortunately, potential sources of sparks were not in short supply: a cigar or cigarette butt in an era when most men smoked; wood-fuelled stoves in the kitchens; substandard or aged wiring; and fireplaces to ward off the chill in drafty old buildings. Each of these sources caused the fiery destruction of at least one of the Muskoka resorts. Then there was arson.

By the middle of the twentieth century, these aging structures were developing a reputation as firetraps. With the ruins of Paignton House still smouldering in the background, an exhausted Winston Gonneau, chief of the Minett Station, told reporters: "None of these old buildings is a surprise when they burn. It's a pain. The fire marshal should close them all."[5] It wasn't a popular sentiment, but it was reflective of the frequency with which Muskoka's resorts were lost to flames.

The lucky resorts that survived neglect, fire, or demolition were generally treated to badly needed modernization during the 1970s and '80s. The Deerhurst Resort we know and love today was born in this era; prior to this it was an aging, rustic hotel that hadn't changed a great deal since the 1930s. Other resorts enjoyed similar, though less dramatic, face-lifts. Painstaking restorations have returned the original spirit to several important properties, such as Clevelands House, Windermere House, and Grandview, making it possible to enjoy their distinct beauty as vacationers in years past would have. They have collectively experienced an astonishing renewal of late, with cottage prices prohibitively expensive, more and more people are opting to enjoy their Muskoka experience from the luxury of a resort. As a result, while only a small portion of Muskoka's summer hotels have survived into the twenty-first century, those that have are once again at the centre of Muskoka's identity.

Chapter 1

WAWA HOTEL

A devastating tragedy struck the WaWa Hotel on the night of August 18, 1923. When the Saturday evening dance was over, guests made their way back to their rooms. Most quickly fell asleep, exhausted from their evening of merriment. Among the handful that remained awake were two men who, as fate would have it, found themselves alone in the rotunda, finishing a late-night hand of cards. At some point, a peculiar light aroused their curiosity. Getting up to investigate, they noticed that the flickering orange glow was coming from under the door leading to the baggage room. The men felt an intense heat radiating from the door and saw thin wisps of smoke curling out from the cracks around the door. *Fire!* Panicked, the men pulled the door open and, to their horror, found the baggage room engulfed in hot flames.

The alarm was immediately sounded. Within minutes, the head of the hotel's fire team had assembled his men and, armed with hoses, they started to attack the now rapidly spreading fire. But with the baggage room being so close to the elevator shaft, containing the inferno proved to be an impossible task. The fire quickly climbed to the upper floors. Staff raced and yelled through the halls, banging on doors to wake the guests and get them to safety. There was no time to save personal belongings.

A brisk wind came off the lake, causing the flames to dance with greater intensity, fanning them like unseen bellows. Within half an

The Wa Wa Hotel, Lake of Bays, Highlands of Ontario.

Courtesy of Muskoka Heritage Place.

In its heyday, the WaWa was arguably the finest resort in Muskoka.

hour the flames had swallowed the entire building. Horrified guests watched as the once-magnificent WaWa Hotel was reduced to hot embers before their eyes. It was the end of a grand and exciting story that had begun two decades earlier, one that saw an isolated stretch of lakefront on Lake of Bays developed into one of the most prestigious resorts in Canada.

In the early 1900s, the owners of the Canadian Railway News Company recognized the appeal that the untouched Lake of Bays would offer to summer vacationers.[1] The shores of the southern Muskoka Lakes were already dotted with industry, cottages, and dozens of competing resorts, and the forests had been rolled back to make way for human habitation. But Lake of Bays remained largely pristine and undeveloped. It was the ideal place to experience the very traits that had made Muskoka famous as a tourist destination a generation earlier: tranquility, crystal-clear waters, and a slice of the Canadian wilderness. The company decided to take advantage of the area's solace and natural beauty by building a luxury resort on Norway Point, just east of Baysville, as a means of increasingly passenger traffic on their rail lines.

Serving as a consultant was C.O. Shaw, owner of the Huntsville Navigation Company and a tireless promoter of tourism in the Lake of Bays area.[2] He had a vested interest in seeing the hotel succeed, since every guest bound for the resort would disembark from trains at Huntsville to board one of his steamers for the final leg of their journey. A thriving summer hotel meant steady business, and so he became an avid supporter of the plan and invested considerable sums of money in it.

When construction began in 1908, the builders' aim was to build an establishment that would continue the decades-old tradition of offering elegant hospitality in the Muskoka Region. None of the earlier resorts, however, compared to the Canadian Railway News Company's magnificent wilderness retreat, which they named the WaWa Hotel — *WaWa* being a Native word meaning "wild goose."

The WaWa was a wood-frame building capable of accommodating three hundred guests. It consisted of a three-storey central section flanked by two-storey wings. A spectacular monument tower, five

Courtesy of Muskoka Heritage Place.

The Wawa was located on a picturesque point jutting out into Lake of Bays. Note the purser's cabin on the wharf. The building has now found at home at Muskoka Heritage Place.

storeys in height, crowned the hotel. The architecturally imposing structure was set dramatically along a stretch of fine, sandy beach. Elaborate wood panelling, charming cedar-shake shingles, striped awnings, fine carpets, and tinkling glass chandeliers added a sense of elegance and refinement. And yet, a relaxed atmosphere prevailed, thanks to comfortable wicker furniture, the softness of potted palms, and a comforting glow radiating from the stone fireplaces. The hotel was also noted for boasting many modern innovations, including a searchlight perched atop the tower that could be seen for miles. The brochures described the light as "a novel and interesting feature new to Canada and very popular in resorts in Switzerland."[3]

The WaWa quickly became the most fashionable place in Ontario to spend one's summer vacation, and it attracted people who wanted both luxury and an assortment of outdoor pleasures. Brochures that depicted seven wild geese flying over the hotel's central tower promised healing waters, fresh air to provide a respite from city smog, and — perhaps in slight exaggeration — no mosquitoes. The promotion was successful, because every year thousands of tourists made the trip from Toronto, Ottawa, Boston, New York, Cleveland, and Philadelphia.

From the moment they arrived, visitors knew they were in for a unique experience. The steamship *Florence Main* would gently glide alongside the dock, where staff and other guests waited to greet old friends and meet new arrivals. There was a sense of community here, as families returned year after year. Porters would bring wagons and wheelbarrows down to the water to carry up the heavy trunks, loaded with enough clothes and necessities to last the summer, to the hotel lobby and then to the individual rooms.

Guests who had the pleasure of staying at the WaWa enjoyed all the myriad comforts that the hotel provided. The dining area was brightly decorated, with white linens and silverware sparkling on the tables as sunlight filtered in from numerous windows. It was widely considered the most attractive and welcoming dining room in any of the Muskoka resorts, and even with enough tables to seat hundreds of guests comfortably and with high walls covered in the finest panelling, it still retained a cozy, comfortable feeling that guests enjoyed.

It wasn't just the dining facilities that were grand, but also the accommodations, said to be unparalleled for luxury in Muskoka. Rooms within the resort were typically booked to capacity, but that wouldn't deter the hotel owners, who knew that the time to earn the majority of the year's income was short, no more than a few months long. To accommodate overflow and entice more guests than the WaWa was designed to host, numerous tents were erected across the grounds. Furnished in the same lavish style as the rooms in the hotel — with white wrought-iron beds, fine cherrywood dressers, and porcelain wash basins — the tents were no less comfortable. True, guests had to fight more mosquitoes at night (despite the claims in the brochures to the contrary) and had a longer walk to the bathroom, but few cared about such minor inconveniences; even wealthy guests didn't mind — it was enough just being in Muskoka.

Muskoka meant relaxation, a slower pace of life than the predominantly wealthy American industrialists who visited were accustomed to. The soft, sandy shoreline was crowded with barefoot children running and playing in the water. Their parents were nearly as carefree, spending

Boat House, Wa Wa Hotel, Lake of Bays District, Highlands of Ontario

Photo courtesy of Muskoka Heritage Place.

The pure, crystalline water of Muskoka's lakes and rivers was one of the main allures of the region, so it's not surprising that guests enjoyed spending a great deal of time cruising up and down the waterways.

their days taking in a game of lawn bowling or tennis or simply relaxing in one of the hotel's many canoes, rowboats, and sailboats. Men played friendly games of baseball against guests from other resorts on Lake of Bays. But the highlight of the week was the Saturday night dance, when everyone descended on the grand ballroom to twirl and sway to live music.

Life at the WaWa seemed so magical that many believed the hotel led a charmed existence. And for several years, it did. But soon enough, problems began brewing below the surface that ensured there would be no happy ending for this fairytale locale. Trouble for the WaWa began in a seemingly innocent manner.

In compensation for his assistance in designing and promoting the WaWa, C.O. Shaw had been promised special accommodations any-time he desired. Over the years, Shaw took full advantage of the offer, coming and going as he pleased, arriving unannounced to enjoy a few days respite before just as suddenly leaving. One time, however, he arrived only to discover that his room had been rented out. Shaw was furious, never once seeing that it was unfair and impractical to have a room permanently set aside on the off-chance he might want to make use of it. All he saw was a broken promise and a personal slight. Red-faced, he stormed out of the hotel, cursing loudly and vowing that he would build a resort of his own that would overshadow the WaWa and drive it into the ground.

Some people might make idle threats to blow off steam, but not C.O. Shaw. He intended to follow through, and in an act of pure spite, the location he chose for his new resort was directly across the bay from the WaWa, on Bigwin Island. The two hotels were destined for a bitter rivalry.

Bigwin Hotel opened its doors in 1920.[4] Newer and more lavish than the WaWa, it inevitably began to draw guests away from its rival. After a few seasons, the WaWa's owners recognized that, unless something was done, Bigwin would prevail in the war of the resorts, slowly starving its competi-tor of its wealthy guests. They couldn't know that the WaWa's death would come more suddenly, like a knife thrust, rather than a slow wasting away.

Though fire was the cause of the demise of many of Muskoka's grand resorts, few succumbed in such a dramatic and tragic manner as the WaWa Hotel.

The Iroquois *approaches the WaWa dock, circa 1915.*

It was almost midnight on the night of August 18, 1923, when the orange glow of fire was first sighted in the baggage room. The cause of the fire has never been determined, but it was suspected at the time that either a carelessly thrown cigarette or friction in the elevator cables which then ignited the lubricating grease could have been to blame. And although the alarm went up quickly, it was still too late; the hotel was constructed with wood walls and frames, and the insulation consisted of burlap and paper. This was all the fuel the fire needed, and it wasn't long before the flames took control, sweeping up the elevator shafts and stairwells.

The staff raced through the hotel, rousing guests from their sleep. Soon, screams of terror echoed through the halls as hundreds of people tried desperately to escape from the now roaring fire. Half-crazed people dressed only in their nightclothes rushed to windows and threw themselves out when they found the stairs and the elevator blocked by the

Courtesy of Ron Sclater.

raging flames. A few short hours before, guests had been joyfully dancing in the ballroom, playing cards or billiards, or enjoying starlit strolls through the grounds. Now, disoriented and confused, they pushed and shoved their way through darkness and smoke, attempting to escape. It was a scene of utter chaos.

While some staff heroically assisted guests to safety and treated the wounded, others frantically fought to control the inferno. George Millan, hotel engineer and head of the staff fire department, bravely led his team toward the raging flames. Unfortunately, the hoses were of poor quality and could do little to control the blaze. Adding to their demise, the pump house soon caught fire and burned to the ground, rendering the hoses useless. All that could be done was to save as many of the 198 guests trapped by the blaze as possible.

As the fire spread, the flames lit up the night sky with an eerie glow that was visible miles away; local residents Audrey Sherwood and Bertha Robinson recalled years later that the fire was "so bright you could pick up a quarter on the ground in Baysville."[5] People from nearby cottages soon flocked to the scene by boat, eager to provide food, blankets, and clothing, and to lend whatever assistance they could in fighting the flames. They couldn't have been prepared for what they found. Columns of blistering fire and thick black smoke streamed into the hot summer sky, as if hell had erupted on Earth. A light breeze swirled, blanketing the surrounding area with acrid smoke. Many watched spellbound, horrified as staff and guests fought personal battles for survival, desperately trying to escape the fire that had transformed the once-proud hotel into a funeral pyre for those unable to escape.

Numerous guests housed on the second floor turned to the windows when they found their escape blocked by flames. Fortunately, their rooms were outfitted with ropes for just such a purpose. After breaking the glass, they were able to slide to safety. As well, WaWa staff, residents of nearby cottages, and employees from other resorts in the vicinity — including Glenmount, Grandview, and even rival Bigwin — were frantically lifting ladders to the windows in order to help guests to safety. Most managed to escape the inferno, but burns and cuts were numerous. Bigwin Inn became a temporary hospital, the bitter rivalry put aside for one night. The crew of the steamships *Iroquois*, *Mohawk Belle*, and *Algonquin* also raced to the scene to render what aid they could.

Though the night was dominated by acts of heroism and sacrifice, there were heart-rending tragedies, as well. A young girl, fourteen-year-old Margaret Bowker (daughter of C.G. Bowker, general manager of the Canadian National Railway), who had just escaped the hellish flames, buried herself into her father's arms, crying tears of joy as she considered herself fortunate to be alive. Then, remembering she had left all her precious jewellery behind, she tempted fate by racing back into the burning building. She never made it back out.[6] Mrs. Emily A. McNally, the sixty-seven-year-old wife of James McNally, vice president of the map-publishing company Rand McNally and Co., was another tragic victim. After a long and exhausting day, she had retired to her room and, because she was a fitful sleeper, had taken sleeping powder to help her rest. By the time the fire broke out, Mrs. McNally was in a deep slumber and apparently heard nothing of the chaos surrounding her.[7]

Trapped in the hotel's tower, and almost forgotten, were the housemaids, whose quarters were directly above the elevator shaft where the fire had started. Screams could be heard echoing across the lake as these young women attempted to escape. They first tried to descend the three flights of stairs, but found their way blocked by a wall of rapidly advancing flames. Retreating back to their tower quarters, some of the maids panicked and threw themselves out of windows in a desperate bid for survival. Witnesses watched helplessly as the young women leaned from the windows, screaming for help, many jumping when at last their courage failed them, plummeting sixty feet to the ground. Sadly, for many of the maids, death by smoke and fire was replaced by one from broken bones and internal injuries.

Finally, a loud groan was heard coming from the building, loud enough to be distinctly heard above the chaos. For a moment, time seemed to stand still, and then, to everyone's horror, the tower collapsed in on itself, and the last panicked, tear-streaked faces at the windows disappeared. It was an image few who witnesses it would ever forget.

The devastating fire didn't take long to consume the entire building. Within forty-five minutes, one of the most lavish resorts in Muskoka was gone. When the smoke cleared, the WaWa Hotel lay in ruins, reduced to a smouldering pile of glowing embers. Searchers combed through the wasteland of ash, searching for bodies. In total, eleven were dead — all women and many of them members of high-society families.[8] In addition, twenty-five others were seriously injured, mostly with broken bones and cuts sustained after leaping from the windows. Several were severely burned. The injured were rushed by steamboat to Huntsville, where a special train was waiting to transport them to Toronto hospitals.

In the aftermath of the tragedy, serious oversights in the resort's design that had contributed to the loss of life and property were discovered. There were no fire bells to rouse the sleeping guests and alert them to the danger, leaving that task to panicked staff members who could do no more than quickly pound on a door and then race on to the next. Firewall partitions proved useless in slowing the racing flames, which, combined with hoses that were completely inadequate to the task, prevented a more orderly evacuation. So, while there was probably no way the fire could have been contained once it had taken hold, these flaws ensured that the night of August 18, 1923, would be a costly one.

When the dead had been buried and stock had been taken of the monetary loss (which was estimated at well over $200,000), the owners announced their intention to rebuild. Staff and guests who had returned every summer for a generation rejoiced at the news, glad to hear that the beloved WaWa Hotel would rise, phoenix-like, from the ashes. Unfortunately, as events unfolded, they would be sadly disappointed. The insurance money simply did not cover the cost of reconstruction, and with the newer Bigwin Inn already biting into profits, the owners never made good on their promise. Instead, the site of the once-grand hotel remained for years a mound of debris from which the remnants of the stone chimneys emerged like fire-blackened headstones.

To add insult to injury, C.O. Shaw purchased the property and used it to support his operations at Bigwin. Since an increasing number of guests were arriving by chauffeur-driven car, he built a garage to house the automobiles while their owners enjoyed the inn's hospitality. He also established riding stables on the WaWa property, as there were none on Bigwin Island.

A vindictive man, Shaw must have taken secret pleasure in ensuring that there would be no revived WaWa Hotel to challenge his resort. The slight he had endured years earlier was finally repaid.

Later, in the 1930s, the land was subdivided into private lots and cottages were built. As a result, most reminders of the once-prestigious resort were soon erased; the ruins were bulldozed, outbuildings rotted away, and the sandy beach was largely submerged during the construction of the Baysville Dam, which raised water levels by several feet.

As the remnants disappeared with the passing of years and those who remembered the hotel became fewer in number, the WaWa was eventually all-but forgotten. But a few people continue to cherish the memory of grand old hotel. Graeme Ferguson, whose Norway Point cottage occupies part of the old WaWa grounds, still has a place in his heart for the resort and is fascinated by its history. Perhaps that's because his property boasts one of only two original WaWa Hotel structures still standing. "There's a beautiful old gazebo from the WaWa on our property, overlooking the lake," he says with a tinge of excitement in his voice. "If you look carefully, you can see all kinds of graffiti etched into it, most with dates. Since the earliest graffiti we can find is from 1911, we estimate the gazebo was built in that year."[9]

The only other remaining building is the purser's cabin, which was located at the end of the WaWa dock, where the steamers would pull alongside and disembark excited passengers. The cabin was removed from the dock and is now at Muskoka Heritage Place in Huntsville, part of a living history museum that recreates a nineteenth-century Muskoka village. In 2004, the building was completely restored to serve as the Fairy Lake Station, one end of the revived Lake of Bays Railway that operates on-site. The building was given new windows, doors, hardwood flooring, interior walls, and ceiling, and a large railway platform was built alongside it, but otherwise it retains its original appearance.

Sadly, these two humble buildings do little to conjure up the majesty of a resort that set the standard for Muskoka hospitality, or to convey the countless magical memories built there by successive generations of summer vacationers. More importantly, they can't possibly express the horror and heart-wrenching anguish of that fateful summer evening in 1923 when the hotel met its sudden and tragic demise.

SEE FOR YOURSELF

The purser's cabin is located at Muskoka Heritage Place (*www.muskoka heritageplace.org*). Standing at the end of the dock belonging to Norway Point Church affords a panoramic view of the point where the WaWa Hotel once stood. While the trademark beach is but a sliver of its former self, the attributes that made this such a glorious site are still evident. To get to Norway Point Church, turn off Highway 117 onto Glenmount Road. When the road forks, stay on the right to reach the picturesque little church.

Make the trip to Dorset and stop in on the Dorset Heritage Museum. The collection includes rare photos and memorabilia from the WaWa, including original floor plans that, incredible as it might sound, were found lining the walls in an area boat house!

Chapter 2

MONTEITH HOUSE

Although Rosseau House (Pratt's Hotel) is regarded as the first hotel on the Muskoka Lakes, another resort can actually claim this title. One can trace the roots of Monteith House, a once-luxurious resort located in the village of Rosseau, back to 1865, several years before Pratt's Hotel would grace the shores of Lake Rosseau.

Monteith House's claim was a tenuous one, however, and just one of the many intriguing aspects of the hotel's history. Over nearly a century, Monteith House helped popularize Muskoka lamb (at one time was a delicacy across North America), inspired several popular songs, and was once owned by the Shopsowitz family of Shopsy's Deli fame.

When John Beal purchased land in the tiny village of Rosseau in 1865, he built a log shanty on the lot. This building served both as his residence and as the post office for the hamlet. A few years later, he was using the cabin as a primitive but welcoming stagecoach inn, catering to traffic along the Parry Sound Road (now Highway 141). At the so-called Ro Seau Hotel, weary travellers got nothing more than a humble meal, a roof overhead to escape the elements, and a warm bed. After many exhausting hours spent riding along rutted roads, however, such simple luxuries would have felt like heaven.

It's hard to imagine that in this small settler's cabin took root the seed of Monteith House, among the most fondly remembered resorts in Muskoka. But that was all years away. Beal was too busy tending to the needs of his guests to forecast the future, and he wasn't ambitious or enterprising enough to envision a luxury resort.

Four years after arriving in Rosseau, Beal up and left. A Mr. Cooper bought the property and continued to operate the cabin as a roadside inn. It was primitive, but business was good nonetheless. Good enough, at least, to justify Cooper building a two-storey frame addition to the rustic inn in 1871. But apparently not good enough for him to want to remain as proprietor, because a year later, Cooper sold the hotel and left town.

The new owner was Scotsman John Hutton, who operated the hotel with the able assistance of his wife, Agnes.[1] Hutton applied for a liquor licence in June 1873, and reaped even greater rewards with the

Monteith House began as a modest roadside hotel built by John Beal in 1865. This image dates to 1876, when it was known as the Portland House, owned by Walter B. Ross.

sale of whiskey and beer to exhausted travellers and local settlers alike. Unfortunately, he didn't live long enough to truly enjoy the fruits of his labours, passing away just a few years after taking ownership.

The hotel then passed rapidly through a number of hands. Walter B. Ross succeeded Hutton, and named the roadside inn Portland House. In 1877, a Mr. Langtree took possession. He in turn sold it to Captain James Kirkland the following year. It was renamed the Kirkland Hotel. The former skipper of the Muskoka steamship *Nipissing*, Kirkland had more experience in navigation than in running a hotel and proved ill-suited to the task.[2]

The revolving door of proprietors finally came to an end on August 22, 1878, when John Monteith purchased the property and lent his name to the hotel. Monteith was born in 1838 on Manitoulin Island (according to his obituary, he was the first European to be born there), where his father was an Indian agent for many years.[3]

While still a young man, John Monteith began a wholesale fruit business that operated throughout much of Ontario. He then branched out to create a prosperous wholesale and retail butchering business. In 1875, he entered the hospitality industry when he opened the Allandale Hotel in what is now Barrie.[4] Three years later, he bought the stagecoach hotel in Rosseau.

Monteith wasn't happy running a mere roadside inn; he had grander ideas in mind. Inspired by the success of H.R. Pratt's majestic Rosseau House, which lured guests from all over North America and put the village of Rosseau on the map as a premier tourist destination, Monteith decided to transform his humble hotel into a first-class resort.[5] To that end, in the autumn of 1878, only weeks after taking ownership, he began construction of a large three-storey addition.

Monteith House proved popular from the start, but its fortunes received a boost with the demise of Rosseau House in a spectacular fire on October 6, 1883. The despondent Pratts couldn't bring themselves to rebuild, choosing instead to leave Rosseau and their pain behind forever. Though surely Monteith took no pleasure in Pratt's loss, it couldn't have escaped him that the end of Rosseau House would be a benefit for his own business. Monteith House would take on the mantle of most

Courtesy of Rosseau Historical Society.

This image clearly shows the position of a much-expanded Monteith House in the heart of the frontier village of Rosseau.

luxurious resort on the lake, and would assume Rosseau House's former role as the focal point of the village's social life. He was confident that many of Rosseau House's guests, who were already familiar with Monteith House, would opt to spent summers at his resort rather than seek out new opportunities elsewhere.

Monteith's predictions proved correct, and only a few short years after the demise of Rosseau House, demand for accommodations at his resort was so high that he was forced to turn potential guests away. Doing so pained him greatly, so Monteith began to envision a new round of ambitious renovations, the first of several that would see Monteith House evolve into a sprawling structure that had little in the way of uniformity, but character in abundance.

The initial round of construction took place in 1886 or 1887 (sources vary), when a large addition, complete with a stately tower and lavishly decorated with gingerbread trim, was built onto the existing structure. Most of this addition was taken up by a billiards room, a trophy room, and a luxurious main lobby. As an avid hunter, Monteith ensured that stuffed animals — prizes from his wilderness adventures, which included

Well-dressed ladies feeding tame bears. Part of Muskoka's appeal to wealthy urbanites was the opportunity to experience the northern wilderness.

impressive deer and moose heads — found their way into these rooms. It's likely they came from the vicinity of his Monteith Hunting Lodge, a rustic sportsman's resort that predated Monteith House by a number of years.[6]

Across the road from Monteith House, a beautiful waterfront ballroom with a wide veranda and a magnificent maple dance floor was built around the same time. In later years this ballroom served as a roller-skating rink, the first in Muskoka. Always offering the best in sporting amenities, Monteith House also boasted tennis courts beside the dance hall, a lawn bowling court, and rowboats for use on Lake Rosseau.

John Monteith had an expansive farm in Rosseau where hay and grain were grown to feed the resort's milking cows.[7] During the 1890s, part of this farm was transformed into a nine-hole golf course, complete with clubhouse, that could be used by both male and female guests. The remainder of the Monteith farm was used to raise a large herd of sheep, providing a ready source of fresh meat for the resort and with which to supply Monteith's wholesale butcher business. In fact, Monteith is widely thought to have been largely responsible for boosting the popularity of Muskoka lamb, which at one time was a must on the menus of fine dining establishments across Canada. Monteith House had its own on-site butcher shop, which much later was transformed into staff lodgings and then, during the 1940s, into motel-style accommodations.

Monteith was an active member of the community, and Rosseau benefited greatly from his generosity. He supported village institutions and charities, and, after the demise of Rosseau House, he allowed the resort to be used for the communal events that Pratt had previously hosted. These included summer bazaars, concerts, dances, and exhibits of the annual fall fair. The grounds became home to picnics and sleighing parties, and he opened the golf course to the public at a time when most resorts ensured their facilities were the sole domain of their high-society guests. Perhaps most memorable, at least in the mind of Rosseau resident E.J. Sirett, were the Christmas parties held in the ballroom. He reflected years later:

> A huge [Christmas] tree … was set up in the Monteith rink. It was a huge barn of a place, high on posts, intended originally for roller skating and dancing in the summer. It was bitterly cold, though two big box stoves were set up … excitement helped keep the children warm. The tree was placed in the centre of the rink, and the children sat around in two circles. As they sat there, they … heard the sound of sleigh bells coming down the hill from the village. Suddenly, the street door opened and … Santa Claus [appeared] in a little cutter, driving before him six prancing reindeer. There were six of the larger boys dressed as reindeer, hung with sleigh bells and [with] antlers fastened on their heads. What a thrill for the children as Santa and his party circled around the Christmas tree.[8]

Monteith was respected and liked by everyone in Rosseau, so they made sure never to make mention of the scandalous events of his social life. To do otherwise would have hurt an already pained man. When

Monteith had first arrived in Rosseau in 1878, he proudly introduced residents to his wife, Mary Ann Wright. It was plain to everyone why he would be proud of her; the women in town marvelled at her grace and style, and she was so beautiful that the men couldn't peel their eyes away. More importantly, the couple seemed extremely happy, both as husband and wife and as parents to their four small children — sons Arthur, Bert, and George, and little Florence, all freckles and curls.

It therefore shocked everyone, Monteith most of all, when Mary Ann deserted her family in 1885. She slipped away in the middle of the night, abandoning her life and her children for the arms of another man, William G. Norton. The couple fled to the United States and neither Monteith nor his children ever heard from Mary Ann again. Monteith was inconsolable for a time, and publicly humiliated, and so his friends and neighbours in Rosseau closed ranks to support him in any way they could.

Monteith later found happiness again when he met and wed Catherine Tobin. Their union was contented and produced five more children,[9] but it sadly wasn't destined to be a long one. In early 1901, Monteith was stricken by some unrecorded incurable disease (quite possibly cancer) and his health declined rapidly. Six months later, on September 1, 1902, he passed away in a hospital in Barrie. It fell to the two eldest sons from his first marriage, Arthur and Albert (who preferred Bert), to take the reins of Monteith House and steer the resort into the twentieth century. To their credit, the resort continued to thrive and, under their guidance, entered its most vibrant, prosperous era yet. It certainly helped that Arthur and Bert were flamboyant and outgoing personalities, well-suited to the hospitality business.

One of the two brothers' greatest contributions to the Monteith House story was to transform the resort into a place known for its lively music and dancing. This transformation began with the hiring of well-known musician and entertainer John G. Strathdee to perform at the resort's ballroom. Though Strathdee wasn't solely employed by Monteith House, the two names soon became all but inseparable. A prolific songwriter, Strathdee composed a number of songs inspired by the atmosphere at Monteith House, but the two most famous were "Rosseau Town" and "Rosseau Town Goodbye," which quickly gained popularity across North America. It became a tradition for staff and guests to gather on the docks and sing these songs as steamships came and went from the resort. Beyond writing songs that eloquently captured the appeal of vacationing at a Muskoka resort, Strathdee helped cement Monteith House's reputation as one of the pre-eminent places on the lakes to dance the night away.

In later years the music evolved but Monteith House retained its popularity. During the 1920s and 1930s, the dance hall swayed to the tunes of the biggest names of the Big Band Era — Count Basie, Duke Ellington, Jimmy Armstrong, and the Dorsey Brothers. Guests from Monteith House and other nearby resorts, as well as cottagers and locals, were thrilled by the opportunity to get dressed up, escort a beautiful woman down to the dance hall, and spend a magical evening spinning and twirling to the best music of the day. Many nights there were as many as five or six hundred people packed into the hall, representing a financial windfall for the resort and creating a buzz that kept it lively and relevant. Forty years after Monteith House had opened for business, it still managed to retain its lustre.

This view clearly shows the development of Monteith House as essentially three separate buildings. Note the dance hall on the left.

Courtesy of Muskoka Lakes Museum.

Both Arthur and Bert died during the 1930s. Their younger sister, Florence, and her husband, Robert John "Jack" Abbs, ran the resort for a brief time, but it wasn't in their blood as it had been for Arthur and Bert. Neither was young, either, and they didn't have the energy needed to carry a resort through the Depression. Reluctant to part with what amounted to a precious family heirloom, Florence finally put the hotel up for sale in 1938. At that time, Harry and Jenny Shopsowitz were searching Muskoka for a resort to purchase. They toured Monteith House, liked what they saw, made an offer, and ended up the proud new owners of one of Muskoka's grandest hotels.

The Shopsowitzes were a Jewish couple who had immigrated to Canada from Poland.[10] Family lore says their love was illicit and not approved by their respective parents. This posed a problem, because they couldn't imagine life without each other, but nor could they sway their parents into giving their consent for marriage. Not to be denied the future together that they dreamed of, Harry and Jenny eloped in 1912 then immediately came to Canada, perhaps fleeing the wrath of their families. Whatever misgivings their parents may have had about the union were proven unfounded, because the marriage was one of happiness — Harry and Jenny were true partners in life, jointly raising a family and later founding two prosperous businesses.

Harry was a hard-working and ambitious man. When he first arrived in Toronto, he got a job handling eggs at Canada Packers. The job involved long hours for little pay, but it allowed him to eventually save enough money to buy a horse and buggy from which he peddled teas and other items on the city streets. The business proved surprisingly profitable, allowing the Shopsowitzes to save enough money to buy a storefront on Spadina Avenue, where they opened an eighteen-seat ice cream parlour in 1921. This little shop evolved into Shopsy's Delicatessen, and set Harry and Jenny on the road to wealth and prosperity.

By 1938, with their deli thriving, the Shopsowitzes began actively looking to purchase a Muskoka resort. Their motivation for entering this new sphere of business was complex, based both on ambition and a deep sense of resignation. "My grandmother was always driven and desperately wanted the family to make something of itself," said Karen Shopsowitz,

Jenny Shopsowitz, who encouraged her husband to purchase Monteith House after noting that there were no vacation destinations in Muskoka that welcomed Jewish travellers. The hotel became the first Jewish-run resort in the area.

Courtesy of Karen Shopsowitz.

who never knew her grandparents, but devoted her film-school thesis to them and the resort they owned.[11] The resulting movie, *My Grandparents Had a Hotel*, is a touching and insightful tribute to a classic Muskoka resort. "My grandmother always had an ambition to run a cottage country resort. It seemed the next step after running a restaurant. It was something she had been encouraging my grandfather to do for some time, and [it] just so happened that Monteith House became available."

But there was more to it than that. By the late 1930s, the Shopsowitzes were prospering as the proud owners of a well-established restaurant. Like many other wealthy business people, they wanted to spend their summers in relaxed luxury in Muskoka. There was one problem: they were Jewish, and at the time Jews were unwelcome at most resorts. It wasn't overt bigotry, but if you called or wrote inquiring about reservations and your name sounded Jewish, you'd find that the resort was booked solid. It never failed, no matter how well in advance you booked, there were no rooms available. It was this prejudice that moved the

Shopsowitzes to consider investing in a hotel, not only as a vacation property for themselves, but also for their friends and associates in the Toronto Jewish community.

When they saw the rambling 150-room hotel facing out onto Lake Rosseau, Harry and Jenny knew their search was over. This was the resort they had been looking for. A cheque for $25,000 changed hands, and Monteith House was theirs.

Despite the new owners and the new openness to Jewish guests, other changes were slow to come to Monteith House. There were few physical alterations made to the hotel but the dance hall still shook from the feet of joyful dancers, and guests — many from Toronto but some from as far away as Buffalo and New York City — continued to enjoy peaceful and pleasurable vacations. Rates were a very reasonable fourteen dollars per week, which included three large meals a day and a full schedule of social activities. The most obvious change was a slight alteration in name: under Shopsowitz ownership, it became the Monteith Inn.

For the first time in its history, Monteith Inn employed a social director, a youthful and outgoing university student with boundless energy, whose job it was to keep guests entertained. "He spent his days and nights making sure guests always had fun. A typical day started at 7:00 or 8:00 a.m. [with] breakfast, followed by calisthenics from 9:00 to 9:30, then lunch and a leisurely afternoon of activities. There were impromptu shows by the lake, and weekly extravaganzas that gave everyone — the guests, the waiters, and even professional dance fans — the chance to show off their talents," relates Karen in the film. Unscripted fun included swimming off the docks, tennis and other sports, carefree walks, countless hours of practising for the weekly shows, and, for the young people, flirting and dating.

Monteith Inn developed a reputation for outstanding food under the Shopsowitzes, and the formal dinner was a highlight of the day. The Shopsowitz family ate with the guests, taking a table near the kitchen so they could keep an eye on both it and the dining room. Jenny was strict about ensuring that guests didn't receive extra portions and would carefully watch as the waiters paraded out of the kitchen with platters laden with food. But the youthful waiters (university students from Toronto, for the most part) were working for tips and knew that a happy guest was a well-paying guest, and so came up with an ingenious means of getting around Jenny's hawk-like gaze. "We would walk out with extra desserts for our customers…. Mrs. Shopsowitz was very short, under five feet tall, so waiters would hold their trays up high so she wouldn't see what was on them," recalled an unnamed former waiter.[12]

Guests of Monteith Inn frequently rented canoes or rowboats from the Swift Marina, which was located beside the resort's dance hall, or booked spots on the marina's eighteen-passenger boat for a cruise to Port Carling or a sunset cruise out onto Lake Rosseau. "Our business was a going concern while Monteith Inn was in full swing. The resort meant a great deal for many businesses in town," reflected Jim Swift, whose parents ran Swift Marina at the time. Though he was only a young boy, he nonetheless has fond memories of Monteith Inn.[13] "I remember the Grand Room in the Hotel. [It] was decorated with all kinds of animal heads on the walls. It was quite an impressive sight. As a young boy, I would sneak into the games room to play ping-pong with my friends until we got kicked out. But most of all, I remember lying in the marina at night in the summer when it would be too hot to sleep. I would just lay there and listen to the music coming from the dance hall … everyone got dressed up for dinner and dancing in those days, the end of the Romantic Era on the Muskoka Lakes."

Another life-long Rosseau resident, Terry Einarson, also remembers the resort from his childhood: "It was one of the truly outstanding hotels in Muskoka, and the guests were all wealthy people. We were kind of in awe of them. The hotel was reserved for overnight guests, but many local boys drank in the beer parlour, which was open to the public. It was the only place in town to get a beer. There were some jobs for local youths, as well. My brothers, Bill and Jim, for example, worked in the hotel kitchen. There was something really impressive about that old place."[14]

Harry Shopsowitz died in 1945, leaving the Toronto deli to eldest sons Sam and Israel ("Izzy"), while third son David took over the management of Monteith Inn. David continued to operate the aging resort, with its creaking floorboards and sagging porch, for a number of years, but he probably recognized that without serious investment the resort's loyal customer base would deteriorate along with the aging structure.

Jenny's death in 1949 allowed David to make an impartial decision about the property, free of nostalgia or compassion for his beloved mother, whose dream the hotel had always been. In light of the prohibitive cost of renovation, as well as societal changes that saw resorts become more open to Jews and rendered strictly Jewish resorts obsolete, David decided to sell. Replacing the Shopsowitz family as owner was Adolph Goodmund, a man with extensive experience in the hospitality industry.

By the time Goodmund took over, Monteith Inn was weary with age. Shifting and settling during the winter months resulted in warped doors that had to be forced open, slanted floors that groaned underfoot, and ill-fitting windows that let in drafts and bugs. Despite constant attempts to deal with problems as they emerged, the building had more than its share of aches and pains.

In many Muskoka resorts, such obvious signs of aging were considered part of the resort's charm as the product of a long, proud history. When the hall creaked and groaned underfoot or when a door refused to open, guests would smile at the thought of their parents and grandparents walking the same tired halls and pushing against the same stubborn doors. But Monteith Inn was different. Decades of tradition had been broken when it had been purchased by the Shopsowitz family and turned into a Jewish resort, and over a decade of continuity was lost again when the Shopsowitzes sold and took with them their Toronto friends and business acquaintances who had formed the heart of the hotel's clientele. Goodmund was therefore forced to rebuild a customer base at the very time that the Muskoka tourism industry was contracting. The resort aged rapidly. It was a mighty struggle, and after only one year in business, the enormity of the task began to set in.

On November 15, 1950, the Monteith Inn had been closed almost two months after Goodmund's disappointing first season. That evening, teenaged brothers Terry and Jim Einarson, and Jim's girlfriend, Helen, were out for a stroll at around 9:00 p.m. when Helen noticed something peculiar. "She saw a funny light in the sky, a red glow. When we looked closer, we realized the Monteith Inn was on fire," recalled Terry sixty years later from his Rosseau home. "We ran into the service station, which was owned by the Gates at the time, told the owners, and one of them — I can't recall whether it was Bill or Bernice — made the call to the village switchboard to alert the fire department."

By a quirk of coincidence, Bill Gates was fire chief of the village's volunteer fire department, and so was first on scene. He had a unique perspective on how the fire developed. His trained eyes saw something unusual: the flames had actually started at two points, at roughly the same time, on either end of the hotel. The only way that could happen, barring the remotest of coincidences, was arson. He watched helplessly for long minutes until the rest of the fire brigade responded. Meanwhile, a call was placed to the Parry Sound Fire Department, and their trucks raced to the scene, as well.

"I remember when the alarm went off, the flames were already filling most of the building. There really wasn't much hope of saving it," recalls Jim Swift, who was thirteen years old at the time. "It was raining that night, but it did nothing to douse the flames. They were fanned by a strong south wind. In fact, the fire was so hot that the square metal shingles on the Monteith Inn roof — each one measuring 12 inches by 12 inches — were glowing red hot and flying off. The wind carried them all over town, starting fires in yards and on buildings. The United church started on fire, for example, but the fire department contained that quickly. I think that if it hadn't been raining, the whole town could have gone up in flames."

Swift didn't have time to marvel at the fiery drama going on in town. His family's marina was only three hundred feet from the Monteith and there was a very real concern that it would be set alight by embers or red-hot shingles carried by the wind. Swift and his family raced against the clock to empty the boathouse of valuables. "We could feel the heat, even at that distance. The walls of the dance hall, which was located between our boathouse and the hotel, were blistering, and we thought it would go up. The heat was so intense that steam was literally rising off our boathouse's metal roof."

Fire trucks arrived and hoses were turned on the flames by desperate men, but the streams of water were futile. Chaos reigned. Men were running toward the fires, and families were fleeing from them. It was dark, but the village was lit with red. Even above the chaos, people could hear the crackle and roar of flames as Monteith Inn was consumed, occasionally punctuated by the crack of rafters collapsing or the crash of walls giving way.

With the fire so well-established and burning so quickly, there was never any real hope of saving the hotel. Instead, the efforts of the Rosseau and Parry Sound fire departments were focused on preventing the flames from spreading to other buildings. In that regard, they were successful, but it must have pained them to watch powerlessly as the Monteith Inn was destroyed. "The fire burned so intensely that by 12:30 it was over and the hotel was on the ground. The building was made of pine and was fifty or sixty years old at the time, so it just went up like a match," said Einarson. "Everyone in town was sure it was a 'Friction Fire' — you know, caused by the friction of the insurance money passing so quickly from the hands of the insurance company to the policy holder. It had to have been intentionally set."

Morning took forever in arriving, but at last a weak sun rose and shone through the cloud of smoke that cloaked the village. Exhausted firefighters and residents took stock of the damage, wild eyes scanning the remains of the resort. Before the fire, it had been a stately place. Now it was in ruins; charred beams and rubble were strewn everywhere, surrounded by mounds of ash and pools of water. While good fortune had spared the village of Rosseau from devastation, fire had destroyed the once-grand Monteith Inn with brutal efficiency — only an east-end wall, stone chimneys, and a few outbuildings remained.

Some sources suggest Goodmund had hoped to open the next year with only the accommodations provided by the remaining buildings, but that seems improbable. With no dining room or kitchen facilities, a limited number of spartan rooms available to rent out, and no recreational facilities to speak of, it's hard to imagine how Goodmund could have opened in 1951 or why anyone would choose to visit. With his experience in the hotel industry, it was more likely he recognized that it would have been prohibitively costly to rebuild and, with no certainty of recapturing past glories, decided to simply pocket the insurance money and put Monteith House behind him. Certainly, the hopes of many villagers that a new resort would rise from the ashes were soon dashed.

"There was really never any thought of rebuilding. The resort business was nearly gone in Muskoka by this point. People wanted cottages, not resorts," explains Einarson.

All that remained was to determine the fate of the various outbuildings that comprised the Monteith House estate. The former butcher shop was sold in 1959 to the Bracebridge Parish of the Catholic church, and after extensive remodelling, enjoyed new life as St. Michael's Catholic Church. Another building became a store and soda fountain operated by Clarence Shaw. And then there was the aged dance hall, which was purchased by the Swift family and stood empty for a number of years before being torn down. "Thirty years earlier, famous big band musicians had played here and stayed in rooms above the hall," remembers Swift. "When we dismantled the building in 1954 or '55, I found boards in those upstairs rooms where band members had carved their names into the wood. There were some famous names on them. I set the boards aside to keep, but they've since disappeared."

When Monteith House burned down, it drew to a close a significant chapter in Rosseau's history and in the lives of many perennial guests, some of whom would vacation in the same room their parents and grandparents had slept in. It wasn't merely a building that went up in smoke and flame, but also the beloved traditions: the sound of a steamship's whistle blasting to announce the arrival of new guests; the relaxation of reclining on the resort's wide porch and watching the sun sparkle upon the waves of the lake; the memories of gentle summer days spent in carefree pursuits; dancing to tunes performed by the biggest names of the Big Band Era; meeting new friends, and getting reacquainted with old ones. Monteith Inn represented a comfortable sense of continuity for guests and villagers alike. Within the span of a few short hours, however, traditions that had taken generations to build were brutally destroyed and lost forever. As a result, the fire didn't just leave a blackened scar in the heart of Rosseau, but also in the hearts of countless people who had grown to love the old resort, quirks and all.

SEE FOR YOURSELF

The only part of Monteith House still remaining is the former butcher shop/staff lodgings, located at the corner of Highway 141 and Short Street. Since 1959, the plain white building has served as a Catholic church, catering to the local congregation. Unfortunately, while undoubtedly historic, the church does little to reflect the grandeur that was Monteith House in its prime. For those interested in a truly intimate look into Monteith House, Karen Shopsowitz's film, *My Grandparents Had a Hotel,* is available through her website at *moviewitz1@me.com.* The short film includes interviews with several former guests and staff, as well as price-less home movies shot at the resort by Karen's father.

Chapter 3

....

ROSTREVOR

Set alluringly within the seclusion of its own private bay and amid the wild beauty of Muskoka — about as far away from the rat race as you could get — Rostrevor was a popular summer resort that was especially beloved by families. Outdoor activities were favoured — swimming, canoeing, tennis, and hiking. There was always something to occupy a child's attention. But no matter how sweaty, dirty, or just plain exhausted you were, you could rest assured that there was somewhere warm and welcoming to return to at the end of the day.

"It had that feeling of going to summer camp, the perfect place for kids and families. The resort had children's programs and children ran loose because it was such a secluded location. Nothing was ever locked," remembers Liz Dobson, who grew up at Rostrevor. "I think my mother had to chase me down every Labour Day to put shoes on this half-wild kid to take her home and make her presentable for school and civilization. That's the special kind of place Rostrevor was: safe, fun, where owners, staff, and guests were like a big family."

It was like that from the very beginning, almost seventy years before the Dobson family entered the picture, when Rostrevor was founded by the matchless work ethic and clear vision of Irishman Arthur Dinsmore.

Dinsmore was born in the Northern Ireland County of Down on April 25, 1839. He was the son of John Dinsmore, who managed

Rostrevor Estate on behalf of its owner, Lord Chesney.[1] Arthur had a privileged upbringing and was blessed with the finest education. Perhaps it was in his father's example, or the aristocratic wealth with which he was surrounded, but Arthur Dinsmore was instilled with a lifelong drive to succeed, to seek out economic security, to establish a place for himself among the well-to-do. To accomplish that goal, he became a chemist, certain in the belief that the esteemed profession would be his entry to high-class society. But while he did well enough to attract the attention of a well-born young woman, Sarah Jane Sheriff, riches escaped him. It become apparent that Ireland could not provide the lifestyle he envisioned.[2]

Like thousands of other immigrants, Arthur was lured by New York City, a bustling metropolis that held out the promise of advancement and wealth. The opportunity that New York offered was like a siren's call that bewitched Dinsmore; in 1869 he settled his affairs, gathered his family, and assembled what belongings he could. They then boarded a ship heading west, along with other eager immigrants. Accompanying him and his wife were two of his brothers, Joseph, a jeweller, and Edward, an engineer. A third brother, Fred, stowed away aboard the ship but, because he had no profession, was not allowed to remain in the United States. He was sent to Canada instead to find his future.[3]

Things didn't work out as planned in New York City, and within a year Arthur had relocated to Toronto, where he briefly operated an eight-acre market garden.[4] He spent two subsequent years as a grain merchant in Meaford, on Georgian Bay. By 1872, however, Arthur had found his way to Muskoka.

We can only assume he was lured there by the promise of free land, as were so many others at the time. He and his wife arrived in what must have seemed an alien land. The Dinsmores found themselves in a place completely unlike the rolling green hills of their homeland or the urban expanse of New York. Here, forests stretched over the rocky countryside for untold miles, unbroken except for countless lakes and the rarest of farms and villages. The density of the undergrowth and the thick forest canopy gave the landscape a claustrophobic, oppressive feel. Nights were black as pitch, and filled with a chorus of strange, sinister sounds. There must have been private moments when they despaired at the harshness of their new wilderness home, but Dinsmore saw opportunity here in Muskoka, and was determined to make the most of it.

For a few years, he continued to serve as a grain merchant in Bracebridge, but he committed most of his time to his Lake Rosseau homestead. A hard-working, industrious man, he devoted himself to the backbreaking job of clearing the land and replacing the vibrant green forest with golden fields of grain. Every day, he left before dawn and didn't stumble exhausted and aching into his cabin until dusk was painting the horizon orange and red. The work seemed endless, but Dinsmore saw real progress. After five years, he had fifteen acres under cultivation and the land was providing ample crops to feed his family. He continued to clear new acreage every year, incrementally adding to his farm. Cutting so many trees also led him into the logging business for a time, selling the trees he cleared to the Clark Sawmill that sat at the mouth of the nearby Dee River. Some logs he sold, others he exchanged for sawn lumber with which he built a large, attractive two-storey home.

By the late 1890s, Dinsmore was considered well-off, at least by the standards of the frontier region in which he lived. But he wasn't getting any younger. The aches and pains associated with hard work lingered longer, and he found himself winded quicker than in his youth. There had to be an easier way to maintain their lifestyle.

Inspiration was just a few short miles away, in the village of Windermere, where two other settlers, Thomas Aitken and David Fife Jr., were prospering as proprietors of thriving summer resorts — Windermere House and Fife House. Dinsmore, always eager to exploit opportunity, decided he would open his home up to tourists, as well, and he named it Rostrevor Lodge, after his hometown in Ireland.

When the lodge opened for business in the summer of 1898, Dinsmore must surely have felt an ember of satisfaction glow within him. Rostrevor was an instant success. Much of its prosperity was owed to the personality of its owners: Arthur was a hospitable host, and Sarah Anne was a refined, warm, and pious woman, a wife devoted to her husband and a hostess committed to the needs of her guests. Her ready smile was one of the most cherished aspects of Rostrevor.

Perhaps more important in attracting guests was the wide, sandy beach, reported to be the largest and most beautiful anywhere on Lake Rosseau. The beach was so central to Rostrevor's identity that advertisements mentioned it above all other amenities. Of course, business was also boosted by the resort's proximity to the village of Windermere, allowing it to take overflow from both Windermere House and Fife House.

In 1903, just a few short years after opening its doors, the inn could accommodate thirty-five guests. This number increased to sixty just a few years later and jumped again to one hundred by 1916.

Things evolved over the decades at Rostrevor, but the one thing that remained consistent was the appeal of its waterfront. For almost a century, the beach was the focal point of life and leisure at the resort.

It was in these early years that the foundations of Rostrevor's longevity were laid. Many of the guests who spent a summer there were so impressed by the hospitality they enjoyed and so taken with the splendid beach that they returned year after year for decades. Some even established traditions that saw third and fourth generation families calling Rostrevor home during the summer months. And in a very real sense it was home; families would have the same rooms reserved for them every year, children ran free, unhindered by rules, and there was a true closeness between guests, born of familiarity and shared experiences.

Between the hours spent catering to guests, Arthur found time to cultivate the fields and raise sheep, poultry, and cattle. The farm was a vital part of the Rostrevor's success, since it meant that the hotel was self-sufficient in vegetables, eggs, milk, and meat.

From spring to autumn there was a seemingly endless stream of tasks to be performed. It was too much for one man to handle, but Arthur was blessed to have the assistance of his four surviving sons: Robert, John, Arthur, and Fred (two others having died young).[5] All played important roles, both on the farm and at the resort, and were clearly being groomed to one day take over when Arthur became too old to keep up with the countless demands. Sarah Anne, meanwhile, was helped with house-keeping and cooking chores by their three daughters.

Arthur Dinsmore died in the autumn of 1912, throwing the carefully cultivated routine at Rostrevor into disarray. His decision to intimately involve his sons in the resort's management from a young age paid off, and things continued without undue interruption, though there can be no doubt his absence was keenly felt by guests and cast a shadow over the resort for a few summers.

Robert, John, Arthur, and Fred jointly carried on the management of Rostrevor, though most of the Dinsmore family lived in Toronto during the winter. Rostrevor, isolated at the best of times and accessible only by steamer, would have been a truly claustrophobic and lonely spot once Muskoka's thick blanket of snow fell, so one can hardly blame them.

The only son to remain at Rostrevor over the winter months was Fred, who for health reasons (presumably a bronchial condition) was encour-aged by physicians to remain in Muskoka's crisp, clean air year-round. It must have been particularly trying for his wife, Isabelle Holt Ester, who came from England and had never experienced the full brunt of a Canadian winter. Enduring the long months of isolation to faithfully stick by her husband was likely made easier by the strong emotional attach-ment she had to the property. Isabelle had warm memories of holidays spent at Rostrevor with her family, and it was here that she met and fell in love with Fred. Their 1910 wedding was held on the picturesque grounds.

The Dinsmore boys, all of whom were skilled carpenters, made many changes over the ensuing years, moving away from the spartan simplicity of Arthur's tastes to something a bit more fashionable and comfortable.[6] Modern sanitation and gas lighting were installed, and a lawn-bowling green, tennis courts, swimming pool, and a small ballroom for dancing were added. Inside the main lodge, a sense of subtle refinement was introduced in the form of gleaming wood floors, twinkling chandeliers, and updated furnishings. It wasn't luxurious by any stretch, but the changes suggested an element of class that was previously absent.

Additional accommodations in the form of a number of cabins were added as Rostrevor continued to grow: at that time, as many as 120 guests could be housed. It was also around this time that one of the resort's trademarks appeared: white painted stones that spelled out H-O-T-E-L R-O-S-T-R-E-V-O-R were placed on the lawn along the lakefront, and greeted guests arriving by steamship for decades thereafter. Despite the updates, the main attraction remained Rostrevor's homey, family-friendly atmosphere.

But the First World War interrupted life at Rostrevor, as all five Dinsmore boys signed up with the 122nd Muskoka Battalion to serve overseas. When they returned at war's end in 1918, the resort promptly ceased to be family owned. The exact circumstances under which Rostrevor changed hands are unknown, and remain contentious among family descendants even today. What's important is that by 1919, in one way or another, Rostrevor ceased to be Dinsmore family property. Its ownership was assumed by two brothers, Major Trump and Colonel Trump. While the Dinsmores went on to other ventures, the family did retain a cottage adjacent to the resort for a number of years, and from it they likely watched as a series of owners came and went over the next two decades. The 1920s and '30s proved to be unsettled ones for Rostrevor.

Road access finally arrived in the late 1920s when Rostrevor Road was built from Windermere. While most guests continued to arrive by steamship, the road made the location less isolated for owners and staff, and made running the resort easier. Unfortunately, if people thought this would result in a period of greater prosperity for Rostrevor, they were in for a shock. At almost the same time as the road was completed, the stock market crashed and threw the world into the dark days of the Great Depression.

The 1930s was a sad decade for Rostrevor, as the effects of the Depression were keenly felt in Muskoka, especially among area resorts. The flocks of tourists no longer materialized each summer, leaving Rostrevor and other hotels starving for business, surviving on desperate hopes that the next year would see a revival of the economy and a return to normalcy. But year after year, such hopes were dashed. It was during this painful era that Art and Joan Bennett entered the picture and provided some much needed stability.

The Bennetts purchased the resort in these troubled times, but it was their good fortune that by the end of the decade a light began to appear at the end of the tunnel. The crushing weight of the Depression began to lift, new jobs were created as the economy sprang back to life, and a sense of confidence slowly began to re-emerge. Business began to rebound, and tourists were returning to Rostrevor.

Then, in 1939, the Second World War erupted in Europe and Canada was sucked into the conflict. What effect would the war have on Rostrevor? Would its newly restored fortunes be undermined by events in far-off Europe? As it turned out, the resort thrived during the war years. Families needed an escape from the terrible news coming from the battlefields, from worrying about loved ones in the armed forces, from running households with husbands and fathers absent, and from the exhaustion of working long hours at factories churning out goods for the war effort. Rostrevor proved to be the ideal refuge from the grim realities of war.

"During the Second World War, while my father was overseas, my mother and I spent four or five summers at the resort. As advancing years take over, I often return to very happy memories of those summers," says Gillian M. Godfrey (née Jill Harris), who was six years old when she spent her first summer at Rostrevor.[7] She continues:

> We took the train from Toronto to Gravenhurst, then went on a steamship called the *Sagamo*, which was located one stop past Windermere. I still remember the anxiously awaited first view of Rostrevor each summer. It was located in what I remember was a large bay and had a lovely sandy beach. There was a long wharf on

one's left as we approached the beach and on the right hand side were what I recall to be high cliffs. At the time, the resort included the hotel and some cottages, as well as some private cottages in the same area.

Most of the guests during the war years were women and children whose husbands and fathers were fighting overseas. Women made up almost the entirety of the resort staff, as well. Gillian recalls that the majority came from Toronto:

> We waited anxiously for mail to arrive a couple of times each week, hopefully with a letter from a loved one overseas. We also looked forward to new guests arriving in case they were friends from last year. We kids always had great fun. We occasionally walked along the cliff side and I remember deserted homes. We thought of them as haunted houses and were quite frightened to go near them.

Gillian also remembers that the water played a prominent role in daily life at the resort, perhaps predictable when one considered the stunning beach was just a minute's stroll from the front door:

> We played in the water a lot, and it was especially suited for children because the water very slowly and gradually dropped off. When we were there, Muskoka chairs sat along the beach, as well as canvas sling-type deck chairs that pinched many fingers and what I would consider something much like the frame of one of today's futon sofas. The latter were very uncomfortable. The resort had rowboats, a pretty nice sail boat. To me, the sailboat seemed quite large. I recall going out in it with my mother and some of her friends and being terrified. We were way out on the lake, it was very choppy and windy and I was sure we were going over. I have disliked sailing ever since.

Rostrevor

Rostrevor was a family resort where priceless memories that lasted a lifetime were made, as these images from the photo album of Gillian Godfrey illustrate. Gillian visited the resort as a child in the 1940s, and those happy days remained fresh and cherished by her seventy years later.

Terrible as it is to say, the war years were good to Rostrevor. The resort thrived. But even after the conflict ended and the men returned home from distant battlefields, Rostrevor continued to ride the wave of success.

The resort became extremely popular with families. The beach was child-friendly, staff kept the youngsters occupied with programmed activities that allowed parents some desperately needed relaxation time, and the location was secluded enough that the young ones were allowed free rein. Adults particularly enjoyed the fact that the children ate in their own glassed-in dining room with dedicated staff attending to them; this allowed parents to enjoy a quiet meal, and meant that those without children did not have their meals interrupted by childish antics.

Largely because of this focus on a family-friendly vacation experience, Rostrevor did good business throughout the Bennetts' lengthy period of ownership, and was still going strong when they sold out to Don and Shirley Dobson in 1965.

The Dobsons were no strangers to Rostrevor or to the Bennetts, as they had been long-time guests, driving up from their home in Toronto every summer for a number of years. When the chance to purchase the resort they had grown to care for came up, the couple jumped at the opportunity.

As Liz Dobson[8] recalls:

> It was an era when the innkeeper was still a real presence at a resort, someone people knew and loved, and my parents enjoyed that…. My parents became close with other resort owners in the area, especially the Aitkens of Windermere. I remember as a child going to Windermere for dinner and eating with Mary Elizabeth Aitken, and being terrified of her because she was such an intimidating woman. We ate in the dining room with the guests. [The] owners were always around, always present. They were part of the resort's personality. Things are different at resorts today. There is no longer the familiar presence of the innkeeper — you don't know who owns and runs them today.

In 1973, Rostrevor was sold to Ian Brown. Brown only kept the resort for a few years before selling out to Jim and Beverley Burton, who changed the name to Rostrevor Beach Resort. The property was aging, and the old lodge built by Arthur Dinsmore — once the heart of the resort — was now only used as a dining room and as staff quarters for the teenaged summer help (due to poor state of repair in the upper floors and because guests were no longer willing to share communal bathrooms).

By this time, accommodations consisted solely of just over a dozen family cottages. If one looked hard enough, signs of age and disrepair could be seen everywhere on the resort; the buildings and amenities were all decades old and in need of updating, but that would have involved especially deep pockets, as the succession of owners discovered firsthand. That said, and despite the fraying that was beginning to appear around the edges, Rostrevor remained vibrant and lively.

Courtesy of Doug Bishop.

Though Rostrevor was starting to show its age by the 1970s, it is not apparent in this postcard from that era. Today, the beach remains as gorgeous as ever, the focal point of life at the resort.

Doug Bishop worked at the resort as a bellhop, groundskeeper, and kitchen help during the 1970s, and has a number of fond memories from his time there:

> I lived in the old main house. All the staff lived upstairs and the room I took must have once been the ... bridal suite of the original farmhouse — it was the largest. All the waiters (in those days it was waiters, not waitresses) and I lived in the front half, which was the guys' quarters. The chambermaids were in the back half of the upstairs. As the groundskeeper, one of my chores was to rake the eight hundred feet of beach every morning.
>
> Also, all of the cottages had fireplaces, and on "change-over" day [Saturdays] I had to clean out the fireplaces, most of which still had hot embers in them [it was a tradition in those days for guests to have a fire their last night, even in the height of summer]. We put them in metal trash cans and later in the evening took the kitchen garbage and ashes to a garbage bin in an old black convertible Pontiac with no brakes. But at least the radio still worked! It never failed, at night you would hear the fire truck siren going to put out the garbage bin at the dump that we had lit up from the ashes.
>
> All the tips were pooled in those days and the money put in a jar at the front desk for guests to see. The tips were later divided equally among the staff. The only exception was when one guest gave Dave Callingham, my friend and "partner-in-crime," a few joints as her tip — we didn't pool these![9]

As so frequently happened, Doug found romance while working at Rostrevor. One summer, a travelling water-ski show called Water Ski Canada, which put on performances at a numerous Muskoka resorts (including Elgin House, Clevelands House, and Windermere House) and private cottages, did a number of shows at Rostrevor. The professional skiers taught guests how to ski, trick ski, and kite fly. Among the skiers was a young woman who caught Doug's eye. He struck up the nerve to approach her; they hit it off, and later became husband and wife. Interestingly, Doug's maternal grandparents also met at a Muskoka resort: she was a guest at Elgin House and he was a lawn-bowling champion hired by the resort to provide lessons. There was just something about the old Muskoka resorts that generated romance.

Jim and Beverley Burton were Rostrevor's final owners. In an effort to revive flagging fortunes, they made what renovations their resources would allow, changed the name to Rostrevor Beach Resort to focus on its best attribute, and hired an experienced hand at the hospitality trade, Moe McGuinty, to take a firm hold of the reins. Ambitious plans were put in place to completely restore the old lodge to its former glory as a way of turning back the clock and presenting guests with a traditional resort experience.

Unfortunately, the economy of the early 1980s took a turn for the worse and the Burtons were forced to shelve their plans. At the same time, it became increasingly obvious that a modern resort needed to be open for all four seasons and to follow the Deerhurst-style model of selling condos onsite to provide supplemental revenue. Faced with this new reality, and without the resources to develop Rostrevor, the Burtons made the difficult decision to close down. The buildings then sat vacant, slowly succumbing to the elements as time took its inevitable toll.

In 1978, Rostrevor had been the site of a Dinsmore family reunion, where more than seventy-five members of the family gathered from all parts of North America. A few years later, when they heard the resort was closed, abandoned, and awaiting demolition, a number of family members made the journey to Muskoka again to see the ancestral property one final time. One of the family members who attended that day was Kelly Dinsmore, and what she saw deeply moved her:

> We wandered around the vacant buildings and it was
> like time stood still from the day when the hotel closed.
> We went into the hotel, and in the main dining room I

remembered the wonderful evening I spent there. We then walked from cottage to cottage. There were newspapers and magazines on the tables in the cottages, all dated the same day, and the furniture remained neatly in place. It was as if people had left in a hurry, leaving everything behind. It was all very eerie, and a very sad experience — a once grandiose place was now deserted.

The grey, abandoned buildings sat forlornly on the shores of Lake Rosseau for a time, as if silently bemoaning their fate. Inevitably, the property was sold and the buildings were torn down to make way for one of the palatial cottages that line the shores of Lake Rosseau, erasing almost all signs of a beloved summer destination of generations of families. Now, the beautiful beach and calm setting is reserved for a single family. For those who remember the joy of summers at Rostrevor, this is deep tragedy.

SEE FOR YOURSELF

There is precious little of Rostrevor left to see, and even then one must view it from the water, as the road to the former Rostrevor property is now a private drive. The bay, of course, is as picturesque and memorable as it is remembered by Gillian Godfrey, and the beach just as inviting and spectacular. It remains quite possibly the largest and finest sandy beach in Muskoka, and when the Township of Muskoka Lakes allowed the resort property to be subdivided for cottages, many viewed this as a lost opportunity to acquire a spectacular public beach. A massive, multi-million-dollar cottage sits on the exact location of the former resort lodge; indeed, the cottage was built upon the lodge's stone foundation. As of 2010, the boathouse remains, though it is of more recent vintage. It's believed that the tennis courts and swimming pool may still be in existence, and perhaps even still used, but neither are visible from a casual viewing from the water.

Chapter 4

DEERHURST RESORT

Deerhurst, often called the jewel in Muskoka's crown, is one of the region's most enduring and prestigious resorts, a property almost synonymous with luxury. The mere mention of the name conjures up images of warm service, elegant surroundings, captivating scenery, and complete serenity. It's a world-class resort, and is routinely listed among the best places to stay in the world.

Bill Waterhouse, a gentleman who represents the third and final generation of Deerhurst's founding family, smiles deeply and with a sense of satisfaction when considering the resort's reputation for hospitality. He was, after all, largely responsible for establishing Deerhurst's atmosphere of elegance during the nearly two decades that it was under his care. "Things weren't nearly so comfortable when my father and grandfather ran the resort," he explains nostalgically. "It was a rustic country hotel then, and guests — wealthy Americans mostly — came to get a taste of 'real' Canadian wilderness. It was a far cry from the glamour of today — guests from even forty years ago wouldn't recognize it anymore. The modern Deerhurst would be beyond my grandfather's wildest dreams."[1]

In a way, Deerhurst was born of a dream. In 1896, high-born Englishman and recent immigrant Charles Waterhouse — Bill's grandfather — had a sudden vision: he would build a summer retreat along a stretch of prime waterfront on Peninsula Lake. Never mind that he had

Courtesy of Deerhurst Resort.

Charles Waterhouse sits (centre) with a group of guests on the Deerhurst steps, 1899.

no experience running a resort; he was certain of success. That's the kind of man Charles Waterhouse was: ambitious, tireless in pursuit of a goal, perhaps a bit stubborn — in short, a visionary.

Charles Wilmot Waterhouse was born in Southampton, England, in 1861. Raised in the sheltered comfort of a wealthy household, he had neither the training nor the disposition of a Muskoka settler. And yet, that's just where he found himself at the age of twenty-two, having left England alongside his brother, Edward. They were both in search of adventure and a fortune of their own making.[2]

The brothers purchased land in Aspdin, on Golden City Lake, west of Huntsville, and despite not being farmers by heart or heritage, appear to have been relatively successful on the homestead. Charles, however, had a lifelong aversion to labour, so it's unlikely he did much farming himself. Instead, to raise money, he sold the timber and tanbark rights to his property. Most of Charles's time was spent in leisure pursuits: hunting, hosting elaborate dinner parties, putting on amateur theatre productions, or playing cricket.[3] He was an island of upper-class English refinement in a sea of barely civilized backwoods.

In 1897, a decade after arriving in Muskoka, Charles met and wed the beautiful and equally well-bred Hylda Hartley, suddenly thrusting the innocent and sheltered young woman into the Canadian wilds. She adapted, however, and was as instrumental in developing Deerhurst as her husband was.[4]

It was around the time of his marriage that Charles had the sudden inspiration to open a resort. The first step in realizing his dream was the purchase of property on the shores of Peninsula Lake. The location was a huge gamble because, while the selected land was undoubtedly picturesque, there was little tourist activity in northern Muskoka at the time, and no guarantee that guests would come knocking.

But Charles was undeterred and pressed on. Next, he bought fifty thousand feet of lumber and hired an expert carpenter, Richard Clarke, to construct the resort buildings. Work began in April of 1896, as soon as the ice had broken up enough to allow scows loaded with the materials to arrive. Deerhurst was an ambitious and expensive undertaking, so, to finance the venture, Charles sold his previous lot and secured the support of wealthy family members back in England. For a time he also had an equal partner, Charles Thomas Simcox, though his role was entirely financial and he played no active part in running the resort.[5]

Deerhurst was intended to be an inn of fine quality, offering comfortable accommodations to an upper-class clientele: an island of refinement and British hospitality in the midst of the wilderness. The three-storey main building that Clarke erected contained eighteen guest rooms, a dining room, a living room, a smoking lounge, and provided a "most enchanting view of the distant hills and charming waters" from a veranda that ran around most of the exterior.

> On entering, one is at once struck by the handsome appearance of the main corridor, deer heads and other trophies of the chase adorn the wall ... on the right you enter a large reception room, which is comfortably furnished, and a handsome piano occupies a prominent

place in the corner. Immediately across from this is the commodious dining room … the bedrooms are all large, well-ventilated, and comfortably furnished.[6]

Deerhurst's size, elegance, and intent put it in marked contrast to most Muskoka resorts, which started as private homes offering modest lodging to summer vacationers and remained modest throughout their existence. Deerhurst also stood out as the first resort to be located on Peninsula Lake, and the first hotel of any size operating anywhere around Lake of Bays. Indeed, a correspondent of the *Huntsville Forester* rightly credited Charles Waterhouse with being "the pioneer in the summer resort house business on these waters."[7]

From the start, the *Forester* sang Deerhurst's praises, as evidenced by a story dated August 14, 1896, several weeks before the resort had opened for business:

> [T]he new summer hotel on Peninsula Lake built by Messrs. Waterhouse and Simcox is just about ready to receive summer guests. The building stands on a commanding site at the entrance to the lake from the canal on one of the most beautiful spots on the shore, nearly surrounded by a grove that can be made in time one of the loveliest retreats in this country. In choosing the site, the proprieties of this summer resort showed excellent judgment and we have no doubt in a year or so it will be the most popular resort for tourists in this part of Muskoka.

The Waterhouses hosted their first guests — a couple from Rochester, New York — a few weeks after this story ran, but even though the main building was not completed, the guests were "entertained in first-class English fashion."

Since Deerhurst's opening rate was $3.50 per person per week, including three meals a day, this couple accounted for the entire first season's seven dollars in revenue. It was hardly the start Charles had hoped for,[8] but things quickly turned around, thanks in large part to the warmth of the hosts and the setting's natural beauty, and by 1898 Deerhurst was filled with tourists. In fact, the demand was so high that some guests willingly erected tents on the grounds when there were no vacancies. Two years later, to keep pace with the demand for accommodations, the Waterhouses added four cottages, "close to the water's edge, and scarcely visible through the labyrinth of trees and branches."[9]

Credit for this rapid success was due largely to the personal magnetism of Charles and Hylda and their tireless efforts to make their guests' stays comfortable. Despite their upper-class origins and strict adherence to British class distinction, Charles and Hylda were approachable and endearing to all their guests, no matter what their background. They were, in fact, the perfect hosts. Charles was remembered for being kind, light-hearted, and entertaining. His all-consuming role was that of the gracious proprietor, tending to his guest's every whim, night and day. And even though she came from a privileged household in England, one in which she had twenty servants at her beck and call, Hylda adjusted remarkably well to the life of a hotelier. She had few formal responsibilities around the resort other than being a gracious hostess and attentive overseer to the staff (who would later affectionately refer to her as "Grammie," because of her motherly nature). Despite residing in conditions that would have been considered rustic among her family and peers back in England, she had a warmth of personality that was felt throughout Deerhurst.

"My grandparents worked non-stop during the summer months, especially since they were the only form of entertainment at Deerhurst," explains Bill Waterhouse:

> They had to be very social to keep the guests enter-
> tained. Grandfather, who originally was an aspiring
> actor, would put on performances. He would also sing
> while Grandma accompanied him on piano. They were
> both really talented performers. Often, the dining room
> would be cleared of tables and chairs for evening dances.
> On some occasions, an orchestra from Huntsville would

Courtesy of Ron Sclater.

An early image of Deerhurst, circa 1906. Presumably a guest marked the room in which he stayed with the X visible in the upper left.

be brought in, but generally the music guests danced to was courtesy of [my grandparents]. They were the only entertainment … for decades, but the guests loved it.

During the day, there were more varied activities to hold one's attention. Guests at Deerhurst enjoyed leisurely, yet casually formal vacations. They might enjoy a game of tennis on the grass court, rowing in one of the skiffs, or strolling through the woods. Starting in 1900, the Huntsville Lakes Regatta Association held its annual regattas at Deerhurst, making for an exciting day of boat and canoe races, swimming contests, and tug-of-wars. This cherished tradition continued well into the 1960s.

Charles also purchased a steam yacht called the *Star* and offered guests cruises of the picturesque lake. After the Pen Lake Golf Course opened in 1912, he would often use the boat to ferry gentlemen across the lake for nine holes of golf. Charles was an avid sportsman and knew many well-heeled guests enjoyed hunting and fishing; it was part of the wilderness experience, after all. With that in mind, he purchased land on Rain Lake in Algonquin Park and would occasionally take interested guests there for a welcome excursion. They would return a few days later,

A romantic view illustrative of the height of Muskoka's resort era. Here, the steamship Algonquin sails placidly past a proud Deerhurst Resort, early 1900s.

proudly holding aloft their catches but eager once more for the comforts of the resort.

Once the last guest of the season had left, Charles and Hylda would pack up their belongings and return to England for the winter, the resort unlocked in their absence, the idea of theft almost unthinkable at the time. They would remain in England until the spring, when they would return to prepare Deerhurst for another season of hospitality. Their first chore when they returned was to jack up the building and even it out, since the building was without a foundation and would therefore shift during the freeze and thaw of winter. Some years the shifting was so bad that the doors couldn't even be opened. It was a side of the Muskoka resort industry that guests never saw. By the time they arrived, the building was once again picture-perfect and the hosts, the hard work of the spring behind them, were once again prepared to play the role of gracious hosts.

Indeed, while Deerhurst had many obvious charms — a beautiful location, peerless comforts, generous portions of fine English cuisine, and the opportunity for recreation — the resort's success rested almost solely on the warmth and hospitality of Charles and Hylda Waterhouse. They *were* Deerhurst, and it was hard to imagine anyone replacing them. But time marches on, and in 1925, sixty-four-year-old Charles, who was beginning to show signs of the coronary disease that would eventually claim his life, decided to retire from the hectic life of running a resort.[10] It fell to their son Maurice to take over the reins of the hotel and guide it through the trying times to come.

Maurice was a child of two worlds. While he grew up in the Canadian wilderness and loved it deeply, he still maintained the bearing, manners, and accent typical of the British upper class, the result of his parents' influence and years spent in a boarding school in England. His childhood was a happy one; he enjoyed the benefits of wealth and the freedom of growing up amidst unspoiled land that had yet to feel the restrictions of civilization. The booming resort provided an exciting background for his youthful adventures.

Then, in 1914, the First World War shattered Maurice's idyllic world. With the world traumatized by conflict, few people wanted to vacation, and Muskoka's tourism industry nearly collapsed. Even the popular Deerhurst felt the pinch, and was almost always empty. Maurice and his brother, Gilbert, like hundreds of thousands of other young Canadian men, signed up to fight on behalf of King and Country. Maurice was a pilot in the Royal Flying Corps (RFC), while Gilbert endured the misery of the trenches as a member of the Kent Regiment of the British Army. Tragedy struck the Waterhouse family in April of 1916 when Gilbert was killed in action, leaving Maurice the sole heir to his father's resort.

When Maurice returned from the fighting, he gradually took a greater role in the operation of the family business. The resort recovered quickly from its wartime stagnation, so it was an easy transition, and when Maurice took over in 1925, Deerhurst was once again booming. The Roaring Twenties were underway; life was faster and more carefree, fashions had changed to match, and wallets got fatter than ever before. Buoyed by such wealth and exuberance, most of the resorts in Muskoka expanded and became more luxurious.

Deerhurst was an exception to the rule, however. Though it prospered, compared with many of its competitors the resort remained quite

Sending postcards from resorts was a tradition, and most of the larger resorts had their own post offices.

modest. This was intentional. Through the years there was little expansion, and despite ongoing improvements designed to keep the facilities up-to-date, efforts were made to keep things "as they were." The emphasis was on providing a consistent vacation experience year after year and not substantially increasing rates. Not surprisingly, the clientele preferred it that way. Everyone and everything fit together into a comfortably familiar pattern. Under Maurice, it remained a relaxed, low-key environment where wealthy guests enjoyed informal cocktail parties in their cottages rather than formal affairs in ballrooms, and where tales of fishing exploits were more likely to be traded than financial insights. Life at Deerhurst might have been sedate and predictable, but it was cherished as such. Guests, staff, and owners formed one big happy family, literally growing up together in many cases.

As Bill Waterhouse explains:

> My father, like my grandfather before him, enjoyed the casual atmosphere of Deerhurst and was loved by everyone who stayed in the resort, young and old alike. He particularly made children feel special when they

vacationed at Deerhurst. In the beginning of the season he would hide tropical seashells at the beach for
the kids to find throughout the summer, and he would
arrange for a party if a kid's birthday happened to fall
during their summer stay. In many ways, he was a big
kid himself.

Unlike his father, who thought menial jobs were beneath an upper-
class English gentleman and had hired staff to do most of the labour,
Maurice threw himself into the task of running the resort and seemed
to enjoy every aspect of it. He relished rolling up his sleeves and sharing in the work, and while he never shied away from manual labour, his
favourite place to be was in the kitchen, preparing meals for the guests.

His efforts paid off with a business that was even more prosperous and popular than it had been under Charles and Hylda's guidance.
Regular guests, the vast majority of whom were Americans, included
such prominent and well-to-do families as the Grands of Grand & Toy
fame, the Shirriffs, known for their jams and marmalades, distillers the
Seagrams, and the Lambrechts and Wadsworths, who included among
them the president of Morgan-Stanley Bank.

While there were certainly more luxurious resorts in Muskoka
— Bigwin Inn, for example, was arguably the finest vacation hotel in
Canada — these wealthy guests chose to forego elaborate balls and the
height of luxury for Deerhurst's more casual, family-friendly ambience
and an opportunity to escape the rigid formality inherent to their social
standing. In fact, most of these families liked the refreshing atmosphere
so much that they returned year after year, and in ever-greater numbers
as their families grew.

Unfortunately, the Depression struck in 1929, destroying the buoyant mood of the past decade. With an economy severely undermined,
the tourism industry slowed to a mere trickle. It was a struggle for most
resorts to even stay in business, and indeed many across Muskoka were
forced to close their doors. Once again, as it had during the First World
War, Deerhurst found itself almost vacant for weeks at a time, but unlike
many of its competitors, it managed to remain open.

A boost to Deerhurst's fortunes came from an unlikely source: the 1934 birth of quintuplet girls in Callander (near North Bay). The Dionne Quintuplets were a world-wide phenomenon, leading to renewed interest in Northern Ontario and drawing thousands of tourists every year, many of whom extended their pilgrimages to "Quintland," with a stay at a Muskoka resort. Since Deerhurst was one of the few that remained open during the dark days of the Depression, and because it was located conveniently close to the newly laid Highway 60, it was fortunate enough to accommodate a great many of these tourists and remain a viable business.

Maurice had his share of personal tragedies. He lost his first wife, Katherine Perry — an American from Kansas whose family vacationed at Deerhurst — a mere eighteen months into their marriage. A few years later, Maurice remarried. Her name was Harriet Barnhardt, and she was also an American (from Grand Rapids, Michigan) whose family similarly summered at the resort. Harriet worked side by side with Maurice for fifteen years, helping run the business and bearing two sons — John and Bill — before passing away in 1944. The death of Harriet shook Maurice, and though he privately wondered why life had to be so cruel, he never let guests see his suffering. In fact, he threw himself into the resort and the needs of guests with a renewed vigour that allowed him to forget the pain and sorrow that had replaced Harriet as his constant companion.

Thankfully, the misery that hung over Deerhurst lifted in 1946 when Maurice fell in love with Jean MacKay and wed for the third time. Jean shared equally in the responsibilities of running the resort, and complemented Maurice perfectly.

"My father loved the social aspects of running the resort, and it was his personality that made Deerhurst so successful, but he wasn't a true businessman," remembers Bill Waterhouse. "It was only because of my mom that they ever made any money. She was an excellent businesswoman and kept tight control of the finances. Whereas my father never put much thought toward the financial aspects, Mom sure did. It was the first time Deerhurst was run as a real business."

Having taken business courses in preparation for joining Maurice at the resort, Jean began carefully balancing operating costs with revenue, yet always ensuring to maintain the high standard of quality for which the resort had always been known.

Physical change came slowly to Deerhurst, as well. The main lodge remained virtually unchanged until 1920, when an addition was built. It consisted of an enlarged dining room with extra guest rooms above.

Despite the fact that hydro arrived in the area in 1932, gas lighting and coal-oil lamps continued to be used for many years. Hot and cold running water arrived a decade later; previously, water had been pumped from the lake and delivered to guest rooms in pails carried by panting staff members. While refrigerators were introduced in the main kitchen in the 1930s, iceboxes remained in cottages for more than twenty years thereafter. At around the same time, bathrooms with chemical toilets were installed in the cottages. There were only two telephones on the property until 1972.

By the 1930s, the cottages — which were added in a gradual, almost unplanned manner from around 1915 until the late 1940s — were the primary accommodations at Deerhurst, with the lodge rooms booked last, mostly for singles or overflow guests.

Guests boarding a steamship from the Deerhurst wharf.

Sadly, one of the cottages was the scene of the most heart-wrenching episode in the resort's 125-year history. It was 1932, and a young married couple with an eighteen-month-old baby girl was vacationing at Deerhurst. The baby was put down in her crib and was soundly asleep, so her parents decided to slip out for dinner in the lodge. Midway through the meal, the alarm was sounded: a cottage — *their* cottage — was on fire. Staff and guests raced to the scene, but the flames had already engulfed the entire building and formed an impenetrable barrier. There was simply no way to rescue the child. The entire resort went into mourning, and the loss shook Maurice so greatly that he refused for almost thirty years to rebuild a cottage on that site.[11]

While Maurice and Jean were the face of the operation, two people, even people as tireless and enthusiastic as they were, couldn't hope to run the resort on their own. They had to have help, and were lucky to have a dedicated and long-serving staff who became part of a summertime family that happily reunited year after year.

Generally, Deerhurst hired between twenty and twenty-five people each year in those days, mostly young women to serve as waitresses, housekeepers, and kitchen staff. Most resided in simple but comfortable accommodations on the inn's third floor and earned a fair wage. Louisa Ford, an elderly Englishwoman, was a long-time cook who helped Deerhurst to obtain its reputation for dining excellence. Exhausted after lunch service, she would settle down in the pantry with a cold bottle of beer and take a sound nap before the dinner rush. Her days didn't end until midnight, so considering her age, Louisa probably needed and deserved the break. Because of her status as cook, it was accepted. The younger girls had a much shorter leash, one that included a firm curfew that had to be abided by.

With the help of countless dedicated staff members, Maurice and Jean guided Deerhurst, modernized but little changed over the years, until 1972, when it passed to the next generation. With older brother John happily engaged in a successful teaching career, it fell to Bill to continue the Waterhouse legacy. Thankfully, he had inherited the best qualities of both his parents — the work ethic and friendly personality of his father, along with the common sense and head for business of his mother. As a result, Bill proved to be the most inspiring of the three generations of owners, and it was he who was responsible for transforming Deerhurst from a rustic country inn into a modern luxury resort offering the finest amenities and with a world-wide reputation for refinement.

Bill, along with his brother, did his fair share of chores while growing up at Deerhurst, including taking wood to the cottages, maintaining the grounds, and selling live bait. Summers were busy with guests, hence the boys had many friends to play with when they were not working; but the winters were long for the Waterhouse family and they were virtually alone, isolated on frozen Peninsula Lake. "There was no one around in the wintertime. I only had one friend and he was miles away, across the Portage," Bill recalls. "All winter I waited eagerly for the summer to come so the guests [would] arrive, because my best friends were American kids who came up every year." Bill put those long, lonely winters to good use, learning self-reliance and discipline while operating a trapline:

> The schoolhouse I went to was a few miles away on the other side of the canal. I had a black lab [retriever] at the time that would meet me at three o'clock and from the time I was twelve we would go off together to tend to my traps. My trapline was five miles long, and I would do pretty good business for myself, selling muskrat, ermine, and mink pelts. And during the summer, I'd sell live bait to the guests. In a way, I was developing my business sense from an early age. I probably always knew I would run Deerhurst one day.

This entrepreneurial spirit only grew as Bill matured. By the time he was fifteen years old, Bill had bought all the boats from his parents and ran the resort's boat rental service. The ambitious young man later attended Ryerson College in Toronto and earned a degree in hotel administration, and then took jobs working in prestigious hotels in Florida and Bermuda. When he returned, he managed the Britannia Hotel on Lake of Bays from 1960 to 1961 — which was, in the words of Bill Waterhouse, "a very swinging place at the time, the one place my parents wouldn't allow me to go to as a teenager." He also developed the nearby Hidden Valley Ski Resort.[12] In 1972, he purchased Deerhurst from his aging parents and set about making his own mark on the venerable hotel:

> When I took over, the resort hadn't really changed since the 1920s. The lodge had only fifteen rooms, and there were only two bathrooms in the entire building. The staff lived on the third floor with the bats. Even including cottages, we could accommodate only about eighty to eighty-five guests, and we were only open in the summer from mid-June to mid-October. I immediately saw the potential in a winterized resort. A decade earlier I was one of the founders of Hidden Valley Ski Club nearby, and with the hills filled with skiers every winter, I knew there was an opportunity to turn Deerhurst into a year-round resort. It was continuous expansion after that, so that by the 1980s we had five hundred staff and seven to eight hundred guests at one time.[13]

Under Bill Waterhouse's guidance, Deerhurst also began a transformation into one of Ontario's most luxurious resorts. Soft lighting, gourmet dining, private whirlpool baths, and fireplaces in every room spoke more to romantics than families. Some of the older clientele were less than pleased with the alterations, but Bill knew that times had changed and the resort was now operating in a global marketplace, and therefore needed to be reinvented with an exciting, vibrant feel.

Further changes came in the 1980s with the addition of conference facilities, a grand ballroom, a piano lounge, and the championship Deerhurst Highlands Golf Course, which was literally carved out of the adjacent wilderness.

Courtesy of Deerhurst Resort.

Deerhurst has long boasted that it has one of the finest golf courses in Muskoka.

When pressed, Bill Waterhouse acknowledges that the achievement of which he is most proud is the resort's unmatched live entertainment program, which, for modern clientele consisting mostly of couples and corporate guests, was a necessity:

> We were known for our great performers. I brought in a world-class pianist, we always hosted the Second City comedians, which included a teenaged Mike Myers, and we had a Vegas-style show, which did performances all over Ontario during the slow winter months, including Roy Thomson Hall in Toronto and even the Grey Cup gala in Montreal. The place was really humming, and we became known as the "Vegas of the North." Among the hundreds of performers who passed through Deerhurst was a very young, very ambitious Shania Twain. I remember Shania vividly. She was a determined, really focused little gal and I'm not surprised by her success. She was a real joy to have on our stage.

Humans

By 1989, Bill Waterhouse no longer found any challenge in Deerhurst. His work had been done, his vision accomplished: Deerhurst was now fully modernized and one of the most elite resorts in Ontario. When an attractive offer to sell was presented to him, Bill didn't hesitate for long. It was sad to say goodbye to a family tradition, but business is business, he reasoned. And so, with a few signatures and a handshake, three generations of Waterhouse ownership ended at Deerhurst. A few months later, as if to underscore that an era in Deerhurst's proud history was drawing to an end, Maurice Waterhouse died at the age of ninety-one. It was a year of conflicting emotions for family, staff, and long-time guests.

Though it would never be the same without the Waterhouse family, Deerhurst endured. What's more, it continued to evolve and define itself, so that today, more than twenty years later, Deerhurst is undoubtedly one of Canada's most impressive resort properties. Set on eight hundred acres of wilderness, Deerhurst allows visitors to appreciate the outdoors while still being in the lap of luxury, blending a year-round natural playground setting with the height of guest comforts and engaging service.

For those who want a more active stay, there are all sorts of exciting activities to choose from: golf, boating, and horseback riding in the summer; dog-sledding and cross-country skiing in the winter. People who are looking for relaxation can unwind at the full-service spa, sink into a bubbling hot tub, or cuddle up to the inviting warmth of a wood-burning fireplace. Simply put, even a few nights at Deerhurst is pure indulgence, the kind not easily forgotten.

Imagine then, what spell it would cast over someone who spent the majority of their lives here? "My father always said that the hotel business gets into your blood, and he was right. It becomes a part of you. It's been twenty years since I sold Deerhurst and it's still a part of me," says Bill Waterhouse from the resort's lounge, as he cast his eyes lovingly over the hotel that had been in his family for more than a century. "You never forget it."

None of those who have experienced the magic of Deerhurst over its 110 years of existence — whether owners, staff, or guests — are able to truly leave the resort behind. They all carry fond memories of their time spent here. Charles Waterhouse, the raconteur and performer, couldn't have dreamed up a better story than that which has played out at the resort he built.

The Deerhurst of today is far more luxurious than that built more than a century ago by Charles Waterhouse, and nowhere is this stunning elegance and majesty more obvious than in the resort's lobby.

SEE FOR YOURSELF

Few would argue about whether a stay at Deerhurst Resort is a mandatory part of the Muskoka experience; the two go hand in hand. Deerhurst successfully captures the relaxed elegance that most modern resorts have tried to achieve, making it pure indulgence. That being said, it's a very different experience than that which would have been enjoyed by earlier vacationers.

Deerhurst has been so extensively remodelled over the past thirty years that very little of historic interest remains. The most notable exception is the main lodge, home to The Lobby Bar and Canada's longest-running live stage production, which dates back to 1981. The lodge is the original Deerhurst, and although it has changed somewhat over the years, it remains a tangible link to the resort's more humble beginnings.

Shamrock Lodge is a throwback to another era, to a time when family-run wilderness resorts abounded along lakeshores, welcoming well-to-do visitors to Muskoka. Times have certainly changed. Far fewer resorts exist today, and those that do bear little resemblance to the ones that kick-started the hospitality industry more than a century ago. They are bigger, more luxurious, and are owned by corporations that run them from distant head offices. From its idyllic location near Port Carling, Shamrock Lodge stands defiant against these trends. The present owners, the Bryant family, run the resort in a manner similar to how their predecessors would have done it a century ago. And therein lies its undeniable charm.

The land upon which Shamrock Lodge sits today, nestled among shaded trees along the shore of Lake Rosseau, was originally part of a large homestead belonging to Irish immigrant Robert Hardcastle Johnston and his wife, Ismay. In subtle but important ways, their legacy is part of the resort's unique character today.

Originally from County West Meath, Ireland, and immigrating to Canada around 1850, Robert arrived in the Port Carling area with his father, Benjamin Hardcastle Johnston, and three brothers in 1860.[1] All of the Johnstons took up land and began the process of clearing forests to make way for fields of crops. Robert's land grant extended from Port

Sandfield Bay east to approximately where the tenth tee of the Muskoka Lakes Golf and Country Club is located today. Family lore suggests he purchased his holdings by paying forty dollars and a white horse to an aged Ojibwe man who resided in the area.[2]

Robert selected the most scenic location upon which to build his home. The land here was smooth and only lightly forested, gently flowing down to a natural sand beach at the head of a placid bay. The view out across the crystal-clear water toward the distant islands was breathtaking, and the tranquility and restfulness of the site providing the perfect cure for exhausting days spent labouring on the farm.

Robert's fine brick home still stands today, serving as the administrative centre and dining facility for Shamrock Lodge. The same qualities that induced him to build his home here are still enjoyed by visitors to the lodge, and provide much of the resort's appeal. The Johnston home has naturally been altered somewhat throughout the years, but many of the original features remain readily apparent, a reminder of the resort's humble roots.

Courtesy of Douglas Johnston.

The original homestead of Robert Hardcastle Johnston, still the focal point of Shamrock Lodge a century later.

92

Robert was a capable farmer, and his herd of dairy cattle made him one of the earliest milk producers in the Port Carling area. Ismay was no less industrious. She worked side by side with her husband on the farm, tended a large market garden, and baked breads and pastries to meet the demands of area cottagers. But though committed to the farm, Robert could hardly help but notice the number of resorts and boarding houses that had begun to spread along the shores of Lake Rosseau in the early 1900s — for a time, even his father, Benjamin, had operated a small resort called Wild Goose Lodge.[3] Because they catered to wealthy tourists who flocked to Muskoka's fresh air and tranquility each summer, even the smallest of these enterprises turned a tidy profit. Robert was impressed. Perhaps he should follow their lead.

Sometime in the early 1900s, Robert started opening up his home to summer guests and referring to his home as Shamrock Lodge, in honour of his homeland. There might only have been one or two boarders at a time, but they paid well for nothing more demanding than a clean room

Robert Hardcastle and Ismay Johnston in later years, clearly enjoying their retirement after a lifetime of adventures wherein they establishing the homestead that would evolve in Shamrock Lodge.

and a soft bed, three square meals a day, and the opportunity to enjoy the landscape that residents such as the Johnstons had long since come to take for granted.

Robert was ideally suited to the role of hotelier. He was gracious and hospitable, endlessly cheerful, and always entertaining, with a seemingly inexhaustible fund of tall tales to share with guests. Perhaps because of these enviable traits, Robert's reputation as a host spread rapidly and the demand for the limited guest rooms at his home rose accordingly. Many of the wealthy families that stayed at Shamrock Lodge in these early years fell so deeply in love with Muskoka that they purchased property from the Johnstons and had Robert build cottages for them. Robert was employed performing annual maintenance on these properties, including opening and closing the cottages in spring and summer, filling icehouses, and shovelling snow during the harsh winters.

Guests were met at the train station in Bala or Gravenhurst and invited aboard Robert's personal steam yacht, the aptly named *Shamrock*, for the final leg of their journey to the lodge. Robert was especially proud of the vessel and would frequently take passengers on sightseeing tours of the lake.[4]

A colourful storyteller, Robert would lace his travelogue with tales of his early years in the bush. He would point out Eagle's Nest, a high, rocky bluff at the mouth of Port Sandfield Bay that was once part of the Johnston property. Here, an eagle with a wingspan of six feet had turned on him with its talons and razor-sharp beak. The terrified settler defended himself with a tree branch, fighting a fierce duel that ended with him bloodied and the eagle dead.

Robert would also relate the story of a large bear that began preying on the Johnston cattle, and how, when he spotted the bear swimming in the lake, he had waded chest-deep into the water to meet the offending predator with an axe. The bear was killed, and Johnston, who was already well-known for his skill at handling an axe, saw his legend grow.[5] Such colourful and dramatic tales added greatly to the experience of sailing on Lake Rosseau, and guests loved the window into wilderness-era Muskoka that they provided.

The Johnstons raised four children, each of whom went on to success in their various fields.[6] But for the Shamrock story, only Alfred is of immediate interest. Alfred Johnston inherited the family farm and Shamrock Lodge in 1934, when eighty-two-year-old Robert finally decided that he could no longer endure the toil.

Alfred realized that he could make more money in the hospitality industry than as a farmer, and so he stopped tilling the soil and planting crops and instead devoted his energies into transforming the home into a small resort. It was an unusual time to take this plunge, since Canada was in the grip of the Great Depression and the ground had dropped out from beneath Muskoka's tourist industry. With money suddenly in short supply, vacationers were not visiting in the numbers seen previously, and most resorts found it difficult to rent enough rooms to stay afloat. Yet Johnston saw not hopelessness but an opportunity to open a resort just when so many others were closing up.

That Alfred's gamble succeeded was due in no small part to his natural wit and charm, inherited from his father, which enchanted guests and served to lure them back summer after summer. One guest, a gentleman named Bob Adamson, came all the way from Florida, faithfully making the long drive from Tampa every year for more than a decade.[7]

At this time, Shamrock Lodge could accommodate forty guests, some within the family home, and the remainder in a four-bedroom cottage annex. It was small, but Shamrock Lodge made up for its lack of size with unrivalled hospitality and a relaxed, home-away-from-home atmosphere. Days were spent reclining in chairs under the sun, paddling in the water, or exploring the woods of the property. For a gentle dash of excitement, the adventurous sort might plunge off a short diving tower that was erected out in Shamrock Bay. As the day ended, guests could be found in front of one of the fireplaces, reading or huddled around Alfred as he regaled them with his tall tales, or outside watching the sunset from the veranda. Guests ate together and the Johnston family joined them, creating bonds that grew with the passage of years. The same relaxed, warm atmosphere remains today, more than seventy years later.

Running a family resort was a labour of love for Alfred, and a family endeavour. For the two or three months in the summer that represent high season, the tireless host and hostess were expected to provide all the comforts of home to the paying public. Typically, Alfred assumed the outdoor responsibilities and Annie oversaw the dining room, kitchen, and guest rooms. Once checked in, the hosts and their three daughters — Wanda, Jean, and Eleanor — devoted their time to fulfilling their guests' needs. Their own lives were put on hold for the summer, but they cherished those hectic, exciting months. The family operated Shamrock Lodge with notable success for fifteen years, carrying on the tradition upon which it was established, while laying the foundations of a modern resort. Their influence is still in evidence today.

In 1947, the aging proprietors sold Shamrock Lodge to a family from Fort Erie. Their ownership was brief and un-noteworthy (so much so that their names have been lost to history), and in 1950 they sold the property to H.B. (Bill) Clinch and his wife, Eve.[8]

Neither Bill nor Eve had any prior experience in the hospitality industry — Bill worked for the Canadian Pacific Railway (CPR) out of MacTier, while Eve was a housewife — but they were enthusiastic, tireless, and hospitable, traits that were ideal for operating a resort. They shared the chores equally: Eve cooked the meals and managed the guestrooms, while Bill was both groundskeeper and handyman.

Bill was often absent, since it was always intended that he continue working for the railway until such time as the resort could support them. Since the tourist season was still essentially limited to the summer months, Eve would lock up the doors each autumn and return to their MacTier home to wait out the winter. This routine continued for almost a decade, until Bill retired from the CPR and was able to focus his attention on the management of the lodge. From that point on, the Clinches remained at Shamrock Lodge year-round and began taking guests into the fall and early winter.

When the Clinches took ownership, the lodge was essentially a large bed and breakfast, and had changed little over the years since Alfred Johnston had established it as a full-time resort. Bill knew that to succeed, Shamrock Lodge would have to be updated and expanded. At that time, there were ten rental rooms in the main house sharing two bathrooms, along with four additional rooms and one bathroom in the "Annex" cabin. Bill began by making major renovations to the main house, later adding further accommodations: two more separate family cottages were built in 1956, as well as a single "honeymoon cabin" in 1959. Finally, in the mid-1960s, Bill tore down "The Annex" and built in its stead a two-storey, winterized, multi-room hotel unit. This greatly increased the number of guests that could be accommodated and made Shamrock Lodge a four-season resort for the first time.

Recreational opportunities expanded in step with increased accommodations. After one very cold and disastrous summer season in which only the hardiest vacationers would brave the chilly waters, an indoor pool was added to guarantee guests good swimming in all weather. In fair weather, Bill would eagerly hop into his launch, the *Billeve*, and take guests on leisurely sightseeing tours of Lake Rosseau. And over time, the Clinches built a close relationship with nearby Port Carling Golf and Country Club, which for the first time allowed resort guests to play on the course. As a result, many avid golfers began to frequent Shamrock Lodge, including some professional players — one summer, the great Canadian golf pro Al Balding was a month-long guest at the resort.

An aerial view of Shamrock Lodge and its environs during the 1960s, clearly showing the beautiful view of Lake Muskoka from the resort.

Bill and Eve established a core of loyal guests who returned year after year; they were more like family than clientele. It must have been painful when, in the 1970s, Eve's health began to decline and the Clinches began to openly contemplate selling the Shamrock. The difficult decision was finally made in 1978, after which Bill and Eve retired to the more hospitable climate of Victoria, British Columbia. The new owners lasted but two short years before selling to Dennis and Murial Bryant in 1980. A new, exciting chapter in the Shamrock Lodge story was about to begin.

At the time of purchase, the resort had been neglected and was badly in need of repair (the previous owners had taken no interest in its upkeep, and Bill Clinch's advancing age had limited his ability to make repairs over the preceding decade), but it was the natural beauty of the area that sold the Bryants on Shamrock Lodge.

With previous experience operating the Bar Head Lodge in Markdale, south of Owen Sound, they knew potential when they saw it and recognized that with time and investment the resort could be extremely successful once more. The family upgraded the lodge and winterized all of the units, adding

This 1980s postcard shows the appeal of Shamrock Lodge: tranquil blue waters, comfortable accommodations, and a relaxed natural setting.

a sauna, whirlpool, and other modern amenities, transforming it into one of the smallest full-service resorts anywhere in Canada. Thirty years and countless renovations later, the resort is still thriving. Sons Tim and Gary now have families of their own and all have joined Dennis and Muriel at Shamrock, continuing a long, proud tradition of family ownership.

In fact, it's this tradition that makes Shamrock Lodge unique. After the recent loss of Tamwood Lodge, Pinelands, and Bangor Resort, Shamrock Lodge now stands alone as the only family-owned-and-operated resort left in Muskoka. "We are carrying on a tradition that the Johnston family started almost eighty years ago, providing an atmosphere for guests that's almost like visiting a friend's cottage," says Tim Bryant with a passion that is contagious, a perpetual smile stretching across his face. Tim is the self-described "front-door man" of the operation, taking over most of the day-to-day activities from his parents, while brother Gary prefers to look after the behind-the-scenes operations. "Being a family-run resort allows us to provide a unique experience unlike what you'd find at a larger resort. We provide the traditional Muskoka experience, which is based on great hospitality and a personal touch."[9]

Here, the ringing of a cowbell calls people in for lunch, guests gather around bonfires until late at night, and end-of-week "award ceremonies" (such as for novice skiers who successfully complete a trip around the bay) are organized to create a sense of camaraderie — all in the best family-resort tradition. Such touches might seem quaint, but it's all part of the resort's unique charm.

When guests arrive at Shamrock Lodge they instantly feel like a part of the family. Tim is always there to greet you upon arrival and to make sure that all your needs are met. He works tirelessly to provide the homey feel that ensures guests are comfortable and ultimately return year after year. Because Shamrock is a full-service, all-inclusive resort, everything is taken care of. All that's left for you to do is to feel the soft, sandy beach beneath your feet. And that's exactly what the Bryants want. "A stay at Shamrock is a cottage experience, but with services thrown in so Mom and Dad can fully enjoy their vacation," Tim explains.

Shamrock Lodge understands that family holidays are important to parents and their children. As such, the months of July and August are devoted to the total family experience. The tranquil setting is transformed into an oasis of activity — canoeing, kayaking, waterskiing, tubing, pontoon-boat tours of Lake Rosseau. And for adults who want to share some quality time alone, there's an all-day children's program (referred to as "Fun Club") for kids four years old and over. There's even a tots babysitting service provided in the mornings.

As one can imagine, the hectic summer months are little more than a blur of activity for the Bryant family. "It's really non-stop, every moment is devoted to ensuring your stay is carefree and that your every need is taken care of," says Tim Bryant. "I interact with guests, I'll spend my days behind the wheel of the boat taking guests skiing or tubing, or conducting scenic boat tours. I don't mind pouring your coffee. It's all about the relationship with the guest."

Though summer is naturally the peak period, Shamrock Lodge remains open year-round, offering winter activities such as snowmobiling, ice fishing, cross-country skiing, and the opportunity to observe deer at a feeding station.

Accommodations at the lodge are all "traditional Muskoka," with comfortable but rustic decor and breathtaking views of the lakeside. There are twenty-four rooms in three styles to choose from: stand-alone cabins, hotel-type accommodations, and semi-detached cabins. Updating the units has been one of the main focuses over the three decades of Bryant ownership, with all of the work being done by the family members themselves. As many as 110 guests can be hosted at one time, a far cry from the modest numbers during the Johnston years.

Even though his sons look after the business now, Dennis Bryant is still very hands-on around the resort and is responsible for making most of the beautifully crafted furniture in the rooms. Muriel is no less involved in the resort, and can often be spotted as she tenderly cares for the plants and flowerbeds around the property. The senior Bryants tend to shun the limelight, but their fingerprints are everywhere. This intimate involvement by the entire family helps create the unique atmosphere at Shamrock. It's tangible somehow, as if you can feel the bond between the family and the resort, and it's just one thing that makes Shamrock so special for the guests — many of whom return year after year.

"That's the greatest joy of running Shamrock Lodge — the relationships you build over the years with repeat clientele," Tim says somewhat wistfully. "It's a great feeling when you're invited to the wedding of someone who's been coming here for ten years or so, since they were a child. It's like you've become a part of their family. And we actually had a young woman working with us a few summers back who had been coming here with her parents every year since she was small. She enjoyed coming to Shamrock so much that she asked if she could spend the season working here. That's pretty special."

For more than seventy years, family memories have been made here. And with a new generation of Bryants being groomed to take over the Shamrock, chances are good that they will continue to be made for many years to come.

Courtesy of Linda Bryant.

Shamrock Lodge is one of very few family-run resorts still operating in Muskoka.

SEE FOR YOURSELF

While changed a great deal over the years, the original Johnston farm home remains and is still an integral part of Shamrock Lodge, serving as the main lobby and dining area. A historic building in its own right, it serves as a reminder of the early years in Muskoka tourism, when large resorts were the exception rather than the norm, and most resorts were little more than homes opened up to guests. For more information on Shamrock Lodge, visit their website at *www.shamrocklodge.com* or call 705-765-3177.

Chapter 6

ROSSMOYNE INN

Rosseau's Rossmoyne Inn was one of the most enduring of the mid-sized resorts in Muskoka, combining warmth, character, and charm into a vacation destination that people would return to year after year, generation after generation. It outlasted many of the more celebrated Muskoka resorts by decades, surviving almost a century of changes in tourism and the hospitality industry to welcome summer guests in a comfortable embrace until it all came to a spectacular end in the autumn of 1971. The inn may be long gone now, but fond memories of what was for eighty years a local landmark remain to this day.

Rossmoyne's story begins almost twenty years before it was even built, with the opening of another resort in the village of Rosseau. In 1869, William H. Pratt came to Rosseau from the United States, bought several village lots, and built a fine summer hotel he named Rosseau House. When it opened for business on July 1, 1870, it became the first resort on the Muskoka Lakes, and paved the way for many others, Rossmoyne among them. Over the next decade, Pratt kept building and improving his business, constantly adding more refinements. The hotel held many socials and concerts that usually ended with dancing, and the Pratts were said to be splendid hosts. They set the standard for other Muskoka resorts, creating expectations in terms of hospitality, refinement, and entertainment.

Sadly, after only thirteen years of business, Rosseau House burned down on October 6, 1883. Left with only sadness, the Pratt's turned their backs on Rosseau and never returned. The hotel was not rebuilt.

The loss of the Rosseau House, which accommodated hundreds of guests every summer, left a void that other enterprising individuals sought to fill with resorts of their own. One of these ambitious men was Rosseau resident Benjamin Beley, who planned to horn in on the area's tourist trade with his Rossmoyne Inn.

Benjamin Sowden Beley, the second son of George and Eliza Beley, was born in 1841 in Liverpool, England.[1] Benjamin's father was a merchant and was involved in an import and export business. His older brother was also a merchant, so it was assumed that Benjamin would also follow in the family footsteps.

But Benjamin's heart was set on becoming a farmer, and he had no intention of entering the world of buying and selling. This decision so angered George Beley that it eventually drove a wedge between father and son that would never be repaired. After realizing he would never find land in Britain, Benjamin and his wife, Lucy, started to look elsewhere for opportunities.[2] In 1867 they moved to Canada, and after a

Benjamin Beley came to Muskoka from his native England in 1867 and established a thriving farmstead. Two decades later, he built Rossmoyne Inn as a mid-sized summer resort.

decade in the village of Ashdown Corners (now a ghost town, the village was located just west of modern-day Rosseau, near Highway 141 and the Old Nipissing Road), they resettled on a farm at Beley Point on Lake Rosseau, where they built a home called Ferncliffe. This home would remain in the Beley family until 1987.

Benjamin Beley erected Rossmoyne in 1887 on land directly across the bay from the village of Rosseau and adjacent to his farm. It was an inspired choice of location; the inn was nestled comfortably between majestic evergreens and sat high atop a hill overlooking the beautiful expanse of the lake. Guests would have enjoyed breathtaking views as they sat on the wrap-around veranda, perhaps contemplating the day's activities. To the south, just offshore, was a picturesque lighthouse that warned boaters of a shoal of rocks. Guests would come to know this lighthouse as a great place to fish. To the east was a marina and the entrance to the scenic Shadow River, a waterway so widely hailed for its beauty that a popular poem was written to sing its praises.[3] And to the northwest was Beley Bay, the north end of Lake Rosseau, where the Beley home was located.

Beley had originally built Rossmoyne as a comfortable summer cottage, but quickly came to realize that there was money to be made in opening its doors to tourists. And in the wake of Rosseau House's fiery demise, there was certainly no shortage of potential guests. Many people who had previously stayed at the grand hotel had come to appreciate the tranquility of the area, and had no desire to vacation elsewhere. Rossmoyne was never intended to be as elegant or as refined as its predecessor, and those guests who wanted such luxuries turned their gaze to nearby Monteith House or Maplehurst. Instead, Rossmoyne was envisioned as a smaller resort where less-well-to-do patrons could feel at home in a comfortable but less formal environment, a place where a personal connection between staff and guests would replace the frills found at larger hotels.

Beley eagerly opened Rossmoyne as a summer resort, but took little hand in its operation. Instead, he turned to Fanita Turner, a family friend from Toronto who frequently spent summers at Ferncliffe, to manage affairs as hostess and innkeeper.[4] Turner proved to be extremely capable

Rossmoyne was a three-storey building that could comfortably accommodate sixty guests.

in the role, and certainly her graciousness and warmth was partly responsible for Rossmoyne's early popularity.

Rooms at Rossmoyne were located in a three-storey building, with two large additional bedrooms in the attic. The inn could comfortably accommodate sixty guests. "The interior was all beautiful old wood, with dark panelling, a beautiful staircase, and polished wood dining tables that made you feel like you were going into a classy place," remembers Margaret Borton, who, as a teenager, worked at Rossmoyne for several summers in the early 1960s. "It was really a beautiful building."[5] A beautiful pump organ occupied the parlour, and when it was played — which was often — its music could be heard all over the property.

Down on the waterfront there was a large dock where guests could enjoy afternoons boating on the lake and paddling their feet in the crisp, clear water. Steamships would nudge up against the dock to disembark their passengers, returning for them weeks or even months later. Alongside the dock was a large boathouse with four second-floor bedrooms where summer staff would stay. A small fleet of rowboats and canoes were moored here for the enjoyment of guests.

Benjamin Beley died in June of 1896, and his youngest son, James Maclennan Beley, inherited the thriving inn.[6] He resided in Memphis, Tennessee, and though he had a summer cottage just south of Rosseau, he had no interest in relocating to Muskoka full-time to take over management of the resort. As a result, he was an absentee owner, leaving the daily operation in the hands of Fanita Turner, even more so than his father had.

James wasn't uninterested, however, and invested heavily in enlarging and updating Rossmoyne to keep pace with rival resorts in the area.

In 1903, James sold Rossmoyne to his younger sister, Ethel, and her husband, Lloyd Dawson. They ran it for another five years before selling it to Joseph Ariss in 1908.[7] Joe and his wife Emma had a long and warm attachment to the property, making them ideal owners. Twenty years earlier, Joe had helped Benjamin Beley build Rossmoyne, while Emma had worked there for years as a maid. The couple had met at the resort

Courtesy of the Rosseau Historical Society.

Rossmoyne Inn included the main lodge, several cabins, and a boathouse which incorporated staff quarters on the second floor. The Beley farm, which remained in the family for over a century, is seen in the distance, across Beley Bay.

and later married there, so it seemed like fate was fulfilled when they signed the deed that brought Rossmoyne into their possession.

A better choice for continuing the traditions begun by the Beley family thirty years earlier could not be had: both Joseph and Emma were locals, had a familiarity with Rossmoyne's operation and its guests, and, most importantly, shared a great affection for the rustic hotel. The transition between owners was flawless, and business essentially went on as it had always done. Rossmoyne would remain in the Ariss family for the remainder of its days. Joe and Emma ran it until 1946, when it was passed on to their son Harold and his wife Jean. Harold and Jean were the first owners not to be residents of Rosseau; after the inn closed each October, they headed to their Orillia home and remained there until the next spring.

Though the Beleys no longer owned Rossmoyne, the family maintained close ties to the resort. This was only natural, in light of the historic connection and because they were close neighbours. Mary Beley, Benjamin's granddaughter and a lifelong native of Rosseau, has many memories of the resort from her childhood in the 1950s. "My first memories of Rossmoyne are from when I was six or eight years old," she recalls. "My aunt and uncle would rent one of the cottages every summer in the late 1940s and early 1950s. They rented Pine Lodge, the cottage nearest the lake one year, then Rosseau View Cottage for several years after that." These cottages, of which there were three in total (Cameron Cottage, Pine Lodge Cottage, and Rosseau View Cottage), had been built by the Arisses a few decades earlier to keep pace with the demand for summer accommodations. Unlike rooms in the inn, which were rented out by the week, the cottages were rented by families for the entire summer. Only two of these cottages remain today: Pine Lodge has been moved off the property and restored, while Cameron Cottage remains at its original site, though it has been so changed that it is now virtually unrecognizable.

Guests in the 1940s and '50s enjoyed relaxing stays, many of them content to do little more than lounge about in wicker chairs. Activities at Rossmoyne were far less varied than those offered by resorts today, and were almost quaint in their simplicity. Guests would spend carefree days picking blueberries, rowing over to a nearby marsh that was a haven for waterfowl and migratory birds, relaxing in the long row of rocking chairs lining the veranda, and hiking over to Mirror Lake and standing atop a cliff that towered so high that hawks would be seen circling below. Guests would often mingle in the kitchen during evening hours, drinking coffee or tea and snacking on cheese and crackers. Many also wanted to help with the dishes, revealing the informality typical of a stay at Rossmoyne.

"I remember the men and boys having a great time playing shuffleboard. Often, my uncle and Dad played against Harold Ariss and his brother Arthur, who lived in Rosseau," recalls Mary. "Also, many guests would paddle a boat over to our sandy beach and swim from it. The properties were so close that guests thought the beach was part of the inn. My Dad didn't mind, though."

The highlight of the summer was undoubtedly the costume party, where all the guests would dress up in outlandish outfits for an evening of dining, dancing, and revelry. Though not guests, the Beleys were always invited.

The veranda was one of the focal points of activity. There was a ping-pong table, a water cooler with a never-ending supply of drinks, and a long row of rocking chairs where guests could sit and rock and catch up with one another's lives. One unique game was known as The Ring. It consisted of a small brass ring with a long string attached, which participants would have to swing and attempt to catch on a hook on one of several poles. The winner was the first person to get the ring on a hook three times.

For teenagers, however, the docks were indisputably the centre of social life. "I remember well sitting on the dock where teenagers who were staying at the inn had plugged a record player into one of the sockets of the lights that shone on the dock at night," remembers Dianne Webster, the daughter of Jean and Harold Ariss. "They danced and sang to the records, and my memory is of wonderful, enchanting times there in the evening, with the lake at peace and water on the dock from all the swimming during the day. It is one of the dearest and clearest memories I have when I hear the songs of that era."[8]

As a summer resort, the staff consisted entirely of seasonal help, mostly young people — four or five per year — from out of town, who spent two or three months living and working on the premises. Margaret Borton was among these enthusiastic teenagers whose youthful energy and friendly personalities ensured guests were well cared for and entertained.[9] "With the exception of one man, the summer staff was all young girls, and we had a great time together. When you're a ... teenager and you're away from home with other girls your age, it's all an adventure and great fun, and you form real companionship with each other," Margaret tells us, before adding with a laugh, "Of course, sometimes our antics — we were young girls after all — would cause Mrs. Ariss some headaches. I remember water skiers from the Canadian National Team came up for a couple of summers because the lake was so calm that they could practise all the time. They were very friendly and took the time to teach us girls and some guests how to ski."

But it wasn't all fun and games for the youthful staff. There was work to be done, and plenty of it. "There were only a few of us, so we did a little bit of everything," Margaret remembers. "Mrs. Ariss was very nice, but she was very strict about appearances — table settings had to be just so, the inn cleaned to perfection, and her woodstove had to be scrubbed spotless. Even at this late date, all of the laundry was still done by hand."

On occasion, during busy periods, a teenaged Mary Beley found herself working at Rossmoyne, as well. "Many local people and cottagers went to Rossmoyne for Sunday dinner, which was too much for the staff to handle, so on long weekends in the 1950s, I worked at Rossmoyne waiting on tables in the dining room."

As its popularity among diners would seem to suggest, meals at Rossmoyne were always exquisitely prepared by Jean Ariss, who cooked exclusively on an old woodstove and who was famed for her Scottish pastries. She used only the freshest of ingredients in her meals: meat, eggs, and dairy were purchased from local farmers, while Harold had a large vegetable garden that supplied the inn's needs. Numerous apple trees provided the fruit for fresh-baked pies. The Beleys, who also had a large garden, would sell raspberries to Rossmoyne in the summer.

Dianne Webster was fifteen when her parents took over Rossmoyne from her grandparents, and while she had previously done some odd work around the inn, her duties now multiplied. She was an employee little different from any of the other teenagers working at the inn, except for the fact her parents were the bosses. "My first job was making the beds in the morning, dusting the rooms, and maybe even emptying the chamber pots. Each room had a wash stand with bowls and pitchers to have a wash in your room, but I don't think they were commonly used because everyone went into the lake," she recounted. "Most of the girls were great, and I made friends of many that lasted over the years. But there was always the awkward fact that the boss was my mother. My mother could be tough on the girls, and it was always hard to hear one of them talking badly about her after they had been reprimanded."[10]

Harold largely left the operation of the inn to his wife and the army of young women she commanded. He contented himself in the role of groundskeeper, but would delight in taking guests out in his boat, the *Happy Days III*, which held up to forty people. Sometimes it would just be a sightseeing jaunt around the lake, but other times Harold would take guests to one of the uninhabited islands for a midday picnic. On occasion, guests would file down to the dock at night for a special outing. Under the pale light of a full moon, Harold would guide the *Happy Days III* out onto the still waters of Lake Rosseau. The only sounds to disturb the evening solace were that of the passengers singing merrily as they cuddled under blankets. Harold would cut the engines and allow the boat to glide up against an island, everyone would disembark, and a roaring fire would be built, and corn roasted in a large iron pot. It was a simple pleasure, but a highlight for many of the guests.

"There was a surprising medley of guests who returned year after year and made the hotel unique," recalls Pearl French, who spent summers there with her husband and three daughters in the 1960s:

One was a doctor from the United States, Dr. Menza, who was a brilliant plastic surgeon who worked on restoring damage done to the soldiers from the Korean and Vietnam wars. He was also a violinist who, along with Ron Whitehouse, the local plumber, would put on little concerts once in a while. I remember some quirky guests, too, like the lady who was allergic to the sun and spent all her time covered up until it was time to go home, and another, an eighty-year-old lady who was a great baseball fan and spent most of her time listening to the ball games.[11]

One of the reasons people kept returning was that the prices were very reasonable; in fact, after a while we wondered why Jean didn't charge more. When asked, Jean said she wasn't out to make money, but was happy to welcome old friends year after year.

Therein lay the secret to Rossmoyne's enduring success. The Arisses, and the Beleys before them, created an atmosphere that made guests feel as if they were being invited into the family home. There was genuine warmth between the owners and their guests, and among the guests themselves, who came to consider one another friends after spending summers together for many years. It was like a big family, and people loved it. Pearl remembers how her family, despite being paying guests, would help chop and pile firewood, waitress at special events, help teach other guests how to water-ski, and lead long hikes. At Rossmoyne, perhaps more than at any other resort, the lines between guests and staff became blurred, creating what in essence was a summer family.

As with any family, staff and guests at Rossmoyne would pull together in times of need, remembers Pearl:

Dr. McQuesten was an old minister from Hamilton — a feisty, almost crippled man with a withered arm and poor eyesight. He loved nothing other than being lifted into his ancient canoe and paddling his way to the mouth of the Shadow River, where he drifted toward the bridge while reading and studying his old bible. One night … Dr. McQuesten didn't return, not even for dinner. As the skies darkened, we all became concerned…. Jean asked everyone with a boat to search the waters. We went everywhere along the shores, into boathouses, up the Shadow River, [but] found no trace of him. Around five in the morning, I gave up. My husband, Fred, dropped me off at the cottage and continued for another hour looking for him. By this time we were searching for an upturned canoe.

Early in the morning, the search resumed. Everyone was exhausted from having been up all night and spirits were deflated by the lack of success. Heaviness weighed on the searchers, certain that it was now a recovery rather than a rescue. Pearl and her husband went up the Shadow River again, holding out hope that perhaps in the darkness and with his failing eyesight the old man had gotten disoriented and had paddled upstream rather than down toward its mouth. As they rounded a bend in the river, their hearts soared as they spotted Dr. McQuesten paddling laboriously.

Pearl remembers:

When we got within his eyesight, he yelled, "What took you so long?" We tied his canoe to our motorboat and made our way back to the hotel. When we arrived at the docks we were greeted by a crowd of very relieved people. Jean told the old minister he should go to his room and rest, but there he was at lunchtime, dressed in his Sunday-best white suit, and said he was fine. Meanwhile, all the rescuers were sick, sore, and exhausted. Later that day, he wanted to go back out in his canoe! What a grand old man!

Despite the affection of loyal patrons who might turn a blind eye to such things, by the 1960s it was obvious to most that the resort was clearly winding down. The guests were almost exclusively older people who had been coming year after year, often since the 1930s. There were few younger guests, which reflected changes in the way North Americans vacationed, and the facilities were growing dated (heating and plumbing had not been updated for decades, and guest rooms still didn't have their own bathrooms). Rossmoyne was living on borrowed time, but even at this late date, the aging property maintained a magical quality.

"The atmosphere was incredible. It was not so much a place as a feeling," says Dianne Webster, who has many fond childhood memories of carefree summers spent at the resort:

> There was just something about the grand old building, with its exquisite woodwork and a huge parlour dominated by a fireplace, around which staff and guests would gather to share a late-night coffee or tea. When I knew it, the attic was closed off and full of bats — believe it or not, it was kind of entertainment for us, chasing around bats that got down into the inn. Many guests, and certainly staff, loved to pick up their tool of choice and attack and bravely be the one to clear the bats out. I have many fond memories of chasing up and down the halls with tennis rackets. Later, I would take my own children up there in the fall when there weren't any guests, and we had a blast. They have cherished memories of the inn just as I do.[12]

With an eye toward the future and the day when they would have to move on from Rossmoyne, Harold and Jean Ariss built a cottage on the property to which they would eventually retire. To finance the construction, they sold off a part of the expansive Rossmoyne property. Unfortunately, Harold died a short time after the cottage was built, never having had the opportunity to enjoy it. His sudden death forced Jean's hand in regard to her beloved resort, and she was faced with a difficult decision. She realized she could no longer run Rossmoyne on her own, and to hire help would have made the property unprofitable. But Rossmoyne was so dear to her heart that she had trouble envisioning life without it. Jean struggled with the decision for a time, but by 1970 she finally realized that the Rossmoyne she loved belonged to the past and had no place in modern Muskoka. The property was sold to a Mr. Wylie and the contents of the building were subsequently put up for public auction.

A year later, in September of 1971, Rossmoyne was demolished. Many Rosseau residents watched with heavy hearts as the building disintegrated in an impressive explosive spectacle, dynamite charges reducing the historic inn to a mound of splinters in seconds. When the dust settled, the witnesses turned their back on the rubble that had once been a proud local landmark and sadly walked away. They knew an era was at an end. The grounds were then subdivided into building lots, and soon all evidence of the resort was gone, another all but lost to history.

Today, most people know nothing about Rossmoyne Inn and its colourful addition to the community's history. It's sad that a unique heritage building, a hotel that was truly spectacular in its day, could so easily be erased to make way for modern development. After speaking to those who knew and loved the resort, our hearts also ached for the loss, and we can only imagine the despair that would have hung heavily over Rosseau in the days after Rossmoyne was destroyed.

Rossmoyne represented a simpler way of vacationing. Though undoubtedly quaint in comparison to modern resorts, those who worked and relaxed here over its eighty years of existence would argue that sometimes simplicity is best. Diane Webster speaks for everyone in Rosseau old enough to remember Rossmoyne when she says, "I feel worse about the loss as the years go by. It was such a special place, a part of so many fond memories for so many people. Now that's all we have of it, and it's tragic."

The view of Rossmoyne as seen from passing steamships, circa 1900.

SEE FOR YOURSELF

Sadly, there is nothing of Rossmoyne left for the public to see. Two of the cabins still exist, one moved off site, but neither is visible from a public vantage point. A plaque dedicated to founder Benjamin Beley, unveiled in 1967, is set within a lakeside rock outcropping at the end of Ferncliffe Bay. Access is only by water. The plaque reads:

BENJAMIN S. BELEY, ONE OF THE PIONEERS IN DEVELOPMENT OF THE MUSKOKA REGION, AND HIS WIFE LUCY ARRIVED IN THE SPRING OF 1867. THEY WERE THE THIRD SETTLERS IN HUMPHREY TOWNSHIP. HIS SON, CHARLES K. BELEY, WAS THE FIRST WHITE CHILD BORN IN THE TOWNSHIP IN 1868. WITH HIS WIFE, AGNES BEAUMONT, HE LIVED TO RENDER OUTSTANDING PUBLIC SERVICE. IN THEIR MEMORY THIS PLAQUE IS PLACED HERE BY C. OLIVER BELEY AND FAMILY.

Chapter 7

PROSPECT HOUSE

It is the 1880s, an elegant era of gentlemen and ladies. The summer sun is high in the sky and the clean northern air welcomes guests. The beautiful sparkling waters of Lakes Rosseau and Joseph are glass-like, showcasing why the area has become a favourite tourist destination, so much so that nearly everyone of wealth seeks to vacation along their shores. As guests pile off of the steamship onto the wharf, they instantly know that the long journey by train and boat has been worth it. Ladies in their gowns and gentlemen in their finery all look forward to their stay at Prospect House, one of the most popular resorts in Muskoka.

Located in the attractive village of Port Sandfield, Prospect House was the destination of choice for many of the idle rich from as far away as England and the southern United States who were searching for solace and escape from the oppressive city heat. In its day, it was one of the elite wilderness resorts in Muskoka.

While Prospect House was built by Enoch Cox in 1881, its foundations were laid years earlier by A.P. Cockburn, the man who was almost single-handedly responsible for making Muskoka a popular tourist destination. Without him, Prospect House and the dozens of other resorts like it on the Muskoka Lakes would not have been possible. Cockburn visited the area in 1865 and, taken by its beauty and charm, was inspired to bring steam navigation to the area.

Cockburn started promoting Muskoka for tourism and settlement. To that end, Cockburn founded the Muskoka Navigation Company and wrote tourist pamphlets to encourage visitors. He also petitioned the government to dig a canal linking Lakes Muskoka and Joseph at Port Carling and another linking Lakes Rosseau and Joseph at Port Sandfield. His promotions worked, and soon tourists were flocking to the area, and resorts began popping up to cater to them.

During the time that Muskoka tourism was being birthed, Enoch Cox was an ocean away, living in his native Stratford-on-Avon, in Warwickshire, England. Cox had a privileged upbringing, the second son of a prosperous timber merchant and barrel-factory owner who leveraged his wealth and status to become a longtime town mayor.

Enoch received a sound education, and even as a youngster, he demonstrated a keen mind, business savvy, and a boundless ambition that would drive him to success — and adventure — later in life. Perhaps he focused his attention on academics and practical pursuits because he was a slight child and frequently ill, so was often unable to engage in the rambunctious games typical of boys.

Rather than work at his father's side, as a young man Enoch went into business for himself, as a draper and proprietor of a general store. Unfortunately, his health — always fragile — began to fail him and doctors recommended a move to the country, where it was hoped the fresh air would help him to recover. As a result, in the late 1850s, Enoch, his wife Sarah, and their young children moved to Wales, where they tried farming for a time.[1]

Not particularly successful, Enoch began to despair. He wanted better for his family and realized farming the rocky hills of Wales, where he had endured high rent, depression in crop prices, and a series of poor harvests, was not the way to go about it. He was, therefore, enticed by the unbridled opportunity that Canada offered, and made the decision to relocate his family. Perhaps with his health restored from the country air, he felt reinvigorated and up for a new challenge. In March 1871, the Coxes left their home in Britain, setting sail for the colonies and an uncertain future.

After a rough, cold crossing plagued with seasickness, they landed at Portland, Maine, and then proceeded by train to Toronto. There the exhausted Sarah Cox said she would go no farther. "I'm not going to the backwoods to be devoured by wild beasts or savage Indians," she reportedly said. Already nearing middle age, the strain of moving from England and the unpleasant crossing had weakened Enoch, also, and so he put up little fight. It was agreed they would stay in Toronto and start a new life in what, even then, was a vibrant, rapidly growing city.

Settling down, they opened a boarding house at 102 Adelaide Street West.[2] Two of their more frequent guests were artist Seymour Penson and cartographer/adventurer John Rogers, who would combine to create *The Guide Book and Atlas of Muskoka and Parry Sound Districts in 1879.*

Everyone who stayed at the boarding house marvelled at the hospitality they enjoyed. "Mrs. Cox was a comfortable, motherly woman, a woman with the warmest of hearts and the kindest of faces," wrote Penson, who would become a lifelong friend to the Cox family. Of Enoch, he wrote, "He was a quiet, pleasant man, with an impediment in his speech, a kind of stammer." Together they created a welcoming environment, and many guests stayed on for weeks or months.[3]

Enoch and Sarah raised two boys and four girls.[4] Edith, the youngest of the girls and the darling of Enoch's eye, "was a pretty young thing with pink and white complexion and a little lisp, a very little one … and very much more vivacity than the average English girl."[5] She gave her heart to the cartographer Rogers, and shortly after they were married they moved to Port Sandfield.

Located on a sandy, thin strip of land between Lakes Joseph and Rosseau, the soil at Port Sandfield was hardly suitable for farming, and yet both Rogers and Penson sent glowing reports back to the Coxes about the area's beauty and potential. At first, Enoch and Sarah dismissed their friends' urgings that they join them in Muskoka, but eventually they became intrigued by the idea. Finally, Enoch could contain his curiosity and a growing craving for adventure any longer. In May of 1871, he and his twelve-year-old son, Edward, travelled to Lake Joseph to stake out a claim and begin clearing land.

Enoch located a lot at the south end of the lake on a pretty bay he named Avon Bay in memory of his hometown in England. Every spring they would head up to Muskoka as soon as the ice had broken up on the lakes (allowing the steamships to begin operating), work all summer cutting down trees and building a home, then return to Toronto and the comforts of home at the first hint of frost.

The Coxes' stay at Avon Bay wasn't destined to last long. In 1874, Seymour Penson offered to sell them his land in Port Sandfield, a plot adjacent to the recently built canal that linked Lakes Rosseau and Joseph. Because of its location, the land had obvious value as an investment: it could be developed in any number of ways. Enoch jumped at the opportunity, and because of that decision, the Cox name would forever remain linked to Port Sandfield.

Starting anew in Muskoka, Enoch and Edward returned to their previous ritual of spending the summer clearing the land and preparing a farm, while Sarah and the girls remained in Toronto to watch over the boarding house. Father and son struggled mightily to make the bush farm work, diligently planting crops and clearing new fields, but it seemed a hopeless task. The soil was sandy, and Enoch could never do more than break even at the best of times. It was disheartening, to say the least.

Frustrated by her husband's futile attempts to establish a profitable farm, and inspired by their success with the boarding house in Toronto, Sarah convinced Enoch that building a wilderness resort was a worthwhile alternative to farming. Enoch agreed, and spent the summer of 1881 building a small summer resort on a picturesque spot on the northeast side of the canal that looked out on Lake Rosseau.

The hotel, named Prospect House, opened in 1882, and could initially accommodate twenty-five to thirty guests. It started out as a plain, barn-like structure of two and a half storeys, with a wide veranda running around its walls — actually, it's quite likely that the hotel *was* the barn, and that Enoch and Edward had repurposed it rather than erecting a new structure.

Its location alongside the canal frequented by steamers meant that the resort had a steady flow of guests, and it was usually booked to capacity. In fact, it was said that guests began to arrive in July of their first summer before the hotel was even truly completed. Enoch and Edward would race to finish building each guest room in turn — just ahead of the arrival of the guests intending to occupy it. There was a smattering of families, but originally the patrons were predominantly wealthy hunters and fishermen who loved the resort because it offered equal access to both Lakes Rosseau and Joseph. Guides intimately familiar with the region, settler and Ojibwe alike, could be hired to lead these sportsmen to the best fishing spots or to areas where they would have the best chance of bagging a prize buck. These early guests wanted adventure, not luxury, so accommodations at Prospect House were originally quite simple: a bed, a washstand with pitcher and bowl atop, and a plain dresser.

Eventually, these sportsmen began to bring their families up to Prospect House, and before long they were staying all summer. By this time, Muskoka had developed into one of the premier holiday regions in North America and what guests had come to expect had shifted accordingly. Guests no longer wanted a rustic wilderness adventure. They now demanded comfort, good food, atmosphere, activities to pass the time, and the opportunity to relax in style.

The success of their retreat drove the Coxes to expand the operation and transform their small hotel into a full-fledged summer resort catering predominantly to the rich. Furnishings in guest rooms became more elaborate in keeping with the status of the clientele. In time, Prospect House became one of the finest and most elegant resorts in Muskoka, and could count among its guests many people of status, including the Earl of Aberdeen and his wife, Ishbel, who enjoyed the Cox hospitality during the summer of 1898. It's also believed that old friend Seymour Penson, who worked extensively as a set designer in Toronto as well as in the United States, may have encouraged many of his theatre friends and acquaintances — actors, singers, and promoters — to vacation at Prospect House. They certainly would have felt right at home, since Sarah Cox was musically inclined and many of the guests at the Toronto boarding house had come from theatrical and artistic circles.

By the late 1890s, the hotel could accommodate 160 guests in luxurious style and comfort. Prospect House boasted a ballroom for dancing, an elegant dining room — the envy of every resort in Muskoka, with gleaming wood and glistening chandeliers — a music room, bowling greens, tennis courts, a sandy beach for swimming and boating, and a host of other features.

The cost for such extravagance was (in 1898) two dollars per day, or eight to nine dollars per week. These rates, among the highest on the lakes, reflected the style and luxury that guests were accustomed to during their stay.

It was often the simplest of pleasures that guests enjoyed the most, such as lounging in shady groves or watching ships pass through the locks from a comfortable chair on the veranda. From 1883, the resort also played host to an annual regatta that drew participants from across the lakes This event was eagerly anticipated by guests, who thrilled at the sleek boats and displays of seamanship.

Enoch died in 1898 while Prospect House was at its pinnacle. Better to go at that time than to have seen all his work, the dreams that he and Sarah had turned into reality, go up in flames in 1916. But between Enoch's death and his beloved resort's fiery demise, there were still plenty of enchanted summers to be played out at Prospect House under the watchful guidance of Edward Cox.

The transition from father to son was seamless and the resort prospered as never before. A vacation at the resort continued to be highly

Prospect House was at its peak in 1913. Three years later it burned to the ground and was never rebuilt.

The steamship Edith May, *owned and operated by John Matheson. The vessel offered guests sightseeing cruises of the lake. The steamship was appropriately named for Matheson's wife, the daughter of Prospect House founder Enoch Cox.*

sought after, and since there seemed to be no keeping up with the demand, additional rooms were routinely added, and by 1910, Prospect House could easily accommodate three hundred guests. Now, she was no longer just one of the more luxurious and prestigious resorts in Muskoka, but also one of the largest. Indeed, one of the employees at the time was a young porter named John Jones, who was so inspired by the Coxes' success that he would go on to open his own resort, Pinelands Resort, near Port Carling, in 1906.[6]

Guests at Prospect House seemed to enjoy the best of all worlds. With hundreds of guests at any given time, and a wealth of activities to partake in, finding good companionship was never a worry. But if you wanted a few moments of quiet reflection, it wasn't hard to find it on a property of nearly one hundred acres. For those who wanted to return to the simplicity of the romantic wilds, gorgeous lakes and dense woods were all around. Others wanted nature to serve more as a back-drop, something to appreciate while reclining on a veranda, cool drink in hand, while enjoying pleasant conversation. Prospect House had that, as well. At the end of a relaxing day, you headed off to the enormous dining room, dressed in a beautiful gown or a formal jacket, for a touch of class and civilization, which the well-heeled guests were accustomed to. Evenings were capped off, depending on your pleasure, with a peaceful stroll along the beach with the sun setting at your back, or twisting and twirling to the music in the ballroom. Prospect House had it all, and thrived as a result.

Luxury and placid summers aside, one of the draws of Prospect House was the unrivalled hospitality and boundless amiability of proprietress Sarah Cox. She was much beloved by guests and townspeople alike, who considered her something of a matriarch. Sarah was known for her deep passion for music. Out of respect for her, Charles Musgrave, the pianist on the steamship *Sagamo*, would play her favourite hymn, "Abide with Me," every time the vessel passed through the canal.[7]

Musgrave was, by all accounts, a fabulously talented musician and a personal favourite of Sarah's, so his services were frequently retained for special events hosted by the hotel. Often these events were so lavish that they were reported in regional newspapers. "On the occasion of Mr.

The Port Sandfield canal opened in 1871. When the steamer Sagamo *passed through, the ship pianist would play "Abide with Me," Sarah Cox's favourite song.*

Ed Cox's birthday, a party and dance was given at Prospect House, Port Sandfield, Saturday evening," announced the *Orillia Times* on May 11, 1914. "The party was a great success owing to the skillful playing of Mr. Charles Musgrave, who puts so much go and spirit into the music that the chairs would have been dancing if they had souls."

But the Coxes weren't all about elaborate parties and refined guests. They were also dedicated to Port Sandfield and, always mindful of their relative affluence, sought to give back to the community as they could. One visible example of their generosity is St. George's Church, a pretty little country chapel they helped fund and which was located on land donated by Enoch and Sarah. Many members of the Cox family are buried in the small adjacent cemetery. In addition, Enoch served as Port Sandfield's first postmaster, and was later succeeded in this role by his son Edward.[8]

Like so many of the grand Muskoka hotels, Prospect House would meet a fiery end. In the early hours of October 15, 1916, a fire broke out and quickly spread through the building. Blessedly, there were no guests in the building at the time. "How the fire started is a mystery," stated the *Bracebridge Herald-Gazette* of October 19, 1916, "but it was soon out of control of the fire fighters, who responded quickly to the scene. The building, which was built of pine, made great material for the flames."

There was little anyone could do to save the building. The next morning, Edward Cox stood on the lawn in front of what had been his hotel, stunned beyond words. Prospect House was no more than charred timber, ashes, and cinders, still warm. Trails of soot and smoke twirled up into the chill autumn sky. The firefighters had expressed their sorrow for not having been able to do more, but by the time they had arrived and began their efforts to control the blaze, it had been far too late. They said that they were lucky to have prevented the towering flames and wind-borne cinders from leaping across to the nearby buildings.

Edward still couldn't get his mind around it. This wasn't just a building reduced to ashes. This was his *life*, his father's legacy, which he had been entrusted to protect. Prospect House had represented the repository of both their hopes and dreams. And now it was gone. The ash-laden air made his eyes water, and through his tears Edward noted

Courtesy of Muskoka Lakes Museum.

Rates at Prospect House were $1.50 per day.

dozens of people around him — firefighters, curious onlookers from the village, his own family — silently moving in and out of the smoky mist like revenants. It all seemed so surreal, like a nightmare.

Forty years of existence, forty summers of fond memories and hard work, had been erased in only a few hours. The loss was devastating and complete. Now Edward Cox faced the painful decision whether to rebuild. Certainly, there were many hoping that he would. "Prospect Point is one of the prettiest spots on the lakes," reported the *Bracebridge Herald-Gazette*, "and the people all over the country would like to see another resort rise in its place."

It seemed to everyone a foregone conclusion that Prospect House would be rebuilt. It was a village landmark, after all, and had been extremely prosperous for decades. But it was not to be. Insurance companies considered country resorts a bad risk and offered Edward Cox a measly eight thousand dollars as compensation for his loss, a mere fraction of the former value of the hotel.

Under such circumstances, rebuilding was clearly not an option. After careful consideration, Cox was forced to admit that there would be no resurrection for the resort where he had spent the past thirty-five years, a resort that he had helped to develop from a wilderness boarding house into one of the elite resorts in Muskoka. The realization left him pained and embittered.

With the demise of Prospect House, Port Sandfield lost its claim to fame. The community became merely a place through which steamers passed on the way to other destinations. The only real winner was nearby Elgin House, which took many of Prospect House's former guests and assumed its role as the pre-eminent resort in the vicinity.

Soon Prospect House was all but forgotten, a mere footnote in the history books. Edward remained in Port Sanfield for the remainder of his years, so it must have been particularly difficult for him to watch as other resorts filled Prospect House's niche and prospered.

Nearly a century after Prospect House was consumed in the inferno, there is little that remains to hint at the village's brush with fame, a time when it was a destination for royals and the well-to-do. We can only imagine those elegantly dressed ladies and their distinguished husbands enjoying the famous hospitality of Prospect House, not to mention the peace and quiet of Muskoka waters free of power boats and jet skis. But we can certainly still appreciate the impact the resort had on the region. The builders of Prospect House were responsible for transforming Port Sandfield from an unimpressive collection of farms to a thriving community, seemingly overnight, and together with the dozens of other summer hotels that were operated over the past 150 years, helped to create the Muskoka we all enjoy today.

SEE FOR YOURSELF

There is sadly nothing to see of the famed resort, though it's worthwhile stopping along the south side of the Port Sandfield swing bridge and, with the photos in this book as comparison, gazing out across the canal to the site where Prospect House once stood. The vantage point you'll enjoy is similar to that of the photographers of yesteryear, making it easier for the hotel to spring to life once again in your mind's eye. St. George's Church, founded in part by Enoch and Sarah Cox, is a short distance to the north and is also worth a brief visit.

Prospect House was built astride the canal linking Lakes Rosseau and Joseph, a picturesque spot and one guaranteed to be well-served by steamships.

Chapter 8

PULFORD HOUSE

Alexander Judson Henderson stuffed his bare hands into his coat pocket and shivered with the chill. The sun shone brightly in a cloudless winter sky, but did nothing to burn away the cold or to lift his dark mood. His eyes gazed lovingly on the resort he had built with his own hands and which he named after his only son. Memories drifted to years past, when the building was filled with summer tourists, when his son rambunctiously played in the dining room and halls.

For a moment, Henderson's mood brightened with the joy of such happy memories. But it darkened just as quickly, for such memories were a thing of the distant past. The resort had not seen a successful summer in years and the youthful energy that once filled the building, even when empty, was absent now that his son had grown up. Instinctively, Henderson knew it was time to move on. It would be up to others to revive Pulford House's flagging fortunes and make Baysville a destination for summer tourists. *And good luck to them*, he thought as he lifted his collar against the cold and turned away from his resort for good.

Pulford House was but one of many resorts that operated in Muskoka, but it stands out for being the only one of any real note to operate in the village of Baysville. Successive owners struggled to put Baysville on the

In this circa 1905 photo, we see Alexander Judson Henderson, his wife Emmeline, their son, Pulford, and a third unidentified male aboard the Monitor. *Henderson built this boat himself and used it to take guests on cruises of Lake of Bays.*

map as a summer tourist destination, but with only moderate success. And yet Pulford House endured for almost fifty years, outliving many of its better-known and more fortuitously located contemporaries. It's sad, therefore, that the hard work, passion, and ingenuity of the various owners, and the decades of priceless summer memories the resort offered, are now all but forgotten.

Many people in today's frenzied society find themselves travelling to the northern parts of Ontario, and Muskoka in particular, in search of solace and relaxation. They are lured primarily by the tranquility of the region's numerous lakes and rivers, and lakefront cottages and resorts have become popular retreats. Things haven't really changed all that much over the past century. Vacationers might get to Muskoka faster today, and upon arrival find the luxuries available that much more impressive, but the allure remains the same. In fact, Muskoka's northern playground was as popular in the early years of the twentieth century, when hundreds of inns and resorts dotted Muskoka's lakes, as it is today.

Baysville, situated on the southern shores of beautiful Lake of Bays, was a latecomer to the resort business. A few settlers opened their homes as destinations for tranquility-seeking vacationers as early as the 1890s, but no resort dedicated to the summer tourist trade emerged until the first decade of the twentieth century. Even then, it only came about by accident.

Baysville was heavily involved in the lumber industry. Several mills were operated in town, and spring log drives passed through on their way down the Muskoka River to Bracebridge. Catering to the mill hands and loggers were several small hotels, which made most of their fortune selling whiskey to these rough-and-ready men. The 1905 decision by the Township of McLean to "go dry," making it illegal to sell or serve alcohol, threatened the livelihood of these Baysville hoteliers. They were understandably irate and fearful for their future, and as a result of the temperance referendum, several threatened to pull up stakes and move on.

Alexander Henderson recognized an opportunity when he saw one and decided to build his own hotel to corner a share of the business. Unfortunately, the irate hotel-keepers who had vowed to leave town unless the temperance vote was overruled proved to be all bluster, and not a single one followed through on their threats. As a result, A.J. Henderson faced stiff competition from the more established businesses; he knew there simply wasn't enough business to support another hotel. Henderson was in something of a predicament. What was he to do with his newly built hotel? He decided to run it as a summer resort. It was a business he was familiar and comfortable with: his parents had operated the Henderson Bed and Breakfast on Lake of Bays for a number of years, catering almost exclusively to summer guests, so he had grown up around the hospitality industry and knew the potential prosperity it offered. It was only natural that he should try his hand at operating a similar establishment.

A.J. Henderson got involved in the business via a circuitous route, though. Always good with his hands, as a young man he moved to Toronto to apprentice as a carpenter. He learned from one of the best; his teacher was central in the development of the once-exclusive Parkdale neighbourhood in Toronto. After completing his training and plying his trade in the city for a while, A.J. returned to Muskoka with his wife, Emmeline Pulford, and put his skills into practice, building cottages along Lake of Bays. Several of these cottages still stand, and include a view of the former resort grounds across the river.

In 1905, A.J. made the momentous decision to change careers from builder to hotelier. He may have been encouraged by his brother-in-law and town founder, William H. Brown, with whom he seemed to be close.[1]

Regardless of how the decision came about, Henderson couldn't have picked a better spot to build — a stretch of land along the Muskoka River in the heart of Baysville that had, until just a few years prior, been home to facilities of the Mickle-Dyment Lumber Company. Henderson recognized the scenic appeal of the location and snapped up the property quickly when he learned it was available. Ugly industrial buildings related to the logging industry were torn down, replaced by a modern hotel that he would take pride in having built himself.

Courtesy of Jean Robertson Dickson.

Early guests arriving by automobile, circa 1910. Note the lift, which took heavy steamer trunks to the upper floor of the hotel.

The resort Henderson constructed was an attractive two-storey structure with more than a dozen guest rooms and a dance floor upstairs. The most unique feature of Henderson's hotel was a winch that lifted heavy steamer trunks from wagons (and later automobiles) parked outside, directly to the upper rooms of the hotel. A.J. also built a boathouse in which he stored the half-dozen rowboats, canoes, and motorboats that he built and rented out to guests. Named Pulford House in honour of A.J.'s son and only child, Pulford Henderson, the hotel opened for business in 1906.[2]

Henderson owned the first gasoline-powered boats in the Baysville area. A pair of elegant launches, the first he named the *Monitor* (one of the first privately owned steam-powered boats on Lake of Bays), and the second, the *Pulford*. These boats was put to good use, ferrying guests to picnics on Burnt Island and taking them on sightseeing tours of the wild shore of Lake of Bays. These excursions were extremely popular among vacationers, many of whom desired a taste of Ontario's "wilderness."

Guests of Pulford House would often picnic on Burnt Island, circa 1910.

Courtesy of Jean Robertson Dickson.

Unfortunately, there just weren't that many guests. Baysville at that time was somewhat isolated from mainstream Muskoka. It could not boast of a train link, and the only means of access was via primitive road or a lengthy boat trip from Huntsville. As a result, despite the undoubtedly natural beauty of the area, the town was slow to develop a tourist trade. Whereas thousands of city-dwellers raced to the more accessible resorts on Lakes Rosseau, Muskoka, and Joseph, the number electing to vacation on Lake of Bays was considerably less — a trickle as opposed to a flood. Even in the best of years the summer tourist season did not exactly provide a windfall for A.J. Henderson.

Nevertheless, Pulford House proved moderately profitable, attracting well-to-do guests from both Toronto and points farther afield. In fact, the first cars seen by wide-eyed Baysville residents were said to belong to guests of the resort. But fortunes plummeted in 1914 when the First World War broke out. The grim reality of war depressed the tourist industry, causing many resorts in Muskoka to cut back on services or close down entirely. Pulford House was no exception, and remained boarded up for the duration of the conflict. Even when the war ended, it took some time for the summer crowds to return to Muskoka. For Pulford House, the recovery period was particularly slow, and the constant vacancies began to wear on its owner. Unwilling to wait any longer, the aging Henderson sold the struggling resort in 1922 and put the hotel industry behind him.

The new owners were John James Robertson, the eldest son of George and Elizabeth Robertson, and his wife, Elizabeth (Libby).[3] Like Henderson before him, Robertson had grown up around the hospitality industry. His parents had opened their lakefront home to guests every summer as early as 1896. Friendly and charming, he was ideally suited to the business and eagerly dove into the role of hotelier.

Inevitably, with a new owner came a new name, and Pulford House became the Robertson Inn. Upon taking possession of the property, Robertson began extensive renovations on the aging and ill-maintained interior, and made several handsome improvements to the grounds. "My father built cement tennis court on the property, the first of their kind anywhere around here. All the tennis courts at

Courtesy of Jean Robertson Dickson.

In 1922, J.J. Robertson purchased Pulford House and renamed it the Robertson Inn. One of the features added by Robertson was concrete tennis courts, the first in the area.

other resorts were grass," recalled Jean Dickson, the daughter of J.J and Elizabeth Henderson, during an interview with the authors in 2000. "A world-class professional tennis player from Gary, Indiana, who vacationed in the area, would often give lessons for the guests at both our resort and Bigwin Inn. In addition to the tennis courts, my father also built a wading pool for kids, because he knew that most of the guests were families with children. He was progressive in many ways. It was funny that his first guests weren't a family, but a pair of trout fishermen from London, Ontario."[4]

Thanks to such novel amenities, as well as the graciousness of the hosts and their tireless devotion to providing a pleasant experience for guests, the Robertson Inn began to flourish. Tragically, J.J. Robertson didn't live long enough to enjoy the fruits of his labours. When he died in August 1933, there was no heir apparent, no one to step forward and continue operating Robertson Inn.[5]

By the 1940s, most guests arrived by automobile. With guests able to more easily reach the Robertson Inn, the resort enjoyed a resurgence in prosperity.

Things looked bleak for a time, until the two Chambers brothers, devoted guests who returned to the Robertson Inn every summer for more than a decade, came to the rescue and purchased the hotel in 1936. They had fallen in love with the property over the years and were determined not to let it go to ruin. So, rather than hoping that the new owners treated the property with respect, they decided to become the caretakers of the Henderson/Robertson legacy. The only significant change the brothers made during their ownership was to change the resort's name once again, this time to Riverview Lodge.

In 1939, another world war erupted and business was again interrupted. But whereas the First World War nearly destroyed the resort, the Chambers brothers found an ingenious method of not only riding out the storm that was the Second World War, but actually thriving during those dark days. Bright men, they realized that with the population working harder than ever to support the war effort, vacations were actually important to maintaining both productivity and morale. So the Chambers brothers approached various munitions plants in Toronto and worked out a deal whereby a small portion of a worker's salary was put aside every week for a summer vacation at the Riverfront Lodge. As a result of this unique scheme, busloads of people from these factories arrived all summer long throughout the six years of the war, providing a prosperity the resort had never before experienced. Vacationers enjoyed treasure hunts, dancing in the second-floor dancehall, boating on the tranquil lake, and other simple pleasures that provided a much-needed break from the stresses inherent in working long hours at the ammunitions plants.

Baysville resident Betty Campbell was a teenager in 1946. One night in April she and her sister and some friends were walking the streets of town, when they noticed smoke shrouding the horizon. "It was early evening, perhaps 7:00 or 8:00 p.m., when we saw smoke coming from the Robertson Inn," Mrs. Campbell remembers. "We were the first people to see it, and we put in the call, I guess you could say. We rang the church bells to sound the alarm, but since we had no fire department in those days, the fire trucks came in from Huntsville and Bracebridge. It was quite exciting."[6]

Being young at the time, the event might have been exciting for Mrs. Campbell, but for many others the destructive power of fire was extremely frightening. There was also a sense of loss; it's always a sad time when a piece of history is destroyed. Soon enough, townspeople had gathered to watch in horror as the flames grew larger and the Robertson Inn slowly faded behind a sheet of orange. Mrs. Campbell recalls that the Walker house was right beside the hotel (an LCBO store stands there as of 2010), and being that close, there was a very real fear that the flames would leap to this building and engulf it as well. Pulling together, the townsfolk raced against time to remove the contents of the home before it was reduced to ashes.

"One of the things rescued from the Walker house was a grand piano, and I remember [that] an elderly gentleman settled himself to play while the fire crews raced to put out the fire," recalls Mrs. Campbell. Thankfully, fire crews, fire rangers from Dorset, and volunteers managed to prevent the fire from spreading to the residence. "Mrs. Walker said that we saved everything except the chicken she was cooking at the time, which by the time she was able to return to her home had been overcooked in the oven."

The Robertson Inn wasn't as lucky. It burned to the ground, and four decades of blissful summer memories were destroyed in less than two hours. Investigators proved that the fire had started when phone and hydro wires had become entangled at the river. As a result, the wires in the boathouse, hotel, and cottages became overcharged with electricity. The fire had started in a linen closet. By the time Mrs. Campbell and her sister noticed the smoke, it was too late to save the hotel. The loss should have come as no surprise, as a fiery demise had been the fate of many Muskoka resorts. Built entirely out of wood, with improper wiring and insufficient safeguards against fire, they were accidents waiting to happen. The hazards were so great, in fact, that many insurance companies refused to cover these hotels.

While the hotel itself was beyond salvage, the firemen had been able to save the outbuildings, including the boathouse, dance hall, three cabins, and the staff quarters. These remnants were purchased by Toronto natives John and Jessie Walsh and turned into a small resort known as Riverside Lodge. Their son, Bob Walsh — seventy-seven years old and still a resident of Baysville at the time of his 2010 interview — fondly remembers the resort and his years growing up among crowds of cheerful guests:[7]

> My parents didn't have any experience whatsoever running a summer resort. My father delivered coal and my mom worked in a war plant. They saw an ad showing the resort for sale and decided to buy it and make a go of it. I can tell you this: there was a lot of work involved in running a resort. My parents were very hard-working people. They spent all their waking hours running the resort during the summer, and when it closed in the winter, my dad often went to Toronto for work. I worked in lumber camps from the time I was twelve to make money for the family, but I returned home every weekend and was put to work by my parents, cutting the grass, bringing in firewood, and loads of other chores. It was tough making a Muskoka resort a success in an age when people could afford to travel overseas or down south.

While the main building may have been destroyed by the fire, Mr. Walsh cautions against the belief that the Riverside Lodge was a shadow of its former self. It remained a busy and beloved resort, its register almost always full during the summer months with as many as sixty guests.[8] Most of the old recreational activities — badminton, horseshoes, canoeing, bicycling — remained, but in addition there was an new twist that brought a renewed sense of excitement to the resort: a dance hall. As Mr. Walsh said:

> The dance hall was always hopping and full on week-ends. It was the place to be. All the guests attended, and some locals, as well. We had a four-piece orchestra, and there was great atmosphere in there. But the dance hall was also used as a dining hall (there was a kitchen in the basement and food was brought up by dumbwaiter), so as soon as dinner was finished there was a mad rush to empty the space and open it up for dancing. It was great fun, though.

Jack and Jessie Walsh only ran Riverside Lodge for five or six years before selling it. The resort continued on under new owners for a few more seasons, but by then the excitement and the profits were gone. With the final demise of the resort in the 1950s, most of the expansive grounds were sold to the Department of Highways, who needed the land to build a new bridge in town. The resort was subsequently demolished. Only one building survived: the eight-room, two-storey former staff quarters that were used by Jean Robertson Dickson (the daughter of J.J. Robertson) as a summer home. Dickson willed her property to the Lake of Bays Township in the hopes that it could be saved in some capacity. Sadly, her dream was not fulfilled. With her death in 2009, the building was demolished, and the final trace of the once-thriving resort was erased. Plans to renovate the home and make it into a small museum of local history, which would have included photos and mementos of Pulford House, sadly came to nothing.

With construction of the bridge completed, the Department of Highways gave the unused portion of the property to the Township of McLean for use as Gristmill Park, which serves as both a tribute to the memory of Pulford House and as a recreational spot for locals and visitors. Its pretty waterline, the feature which inspired A.J. Henderson to build a resort here in the first place a century ago, will undoubtedly be enjoyed by people for many more generations. But sadly, of Henderson's dream, nothing remains but fading memories in the minds of a few aging townsfolk.

SEE FOR YOURSELF

Gristmill Park offers a pleasant stroll through the grounds once occupied by Pulford House, but unfortunately there's little here to hint at the bustle of activity that one would have witnessed while the resort was in its prime. Watch for an information plaque alongside a grindstone from a former mill. Gristmill Park is located along Highway 117, in the heart of Baysville, astride the Muskoka River.

Chapter 9

. . . .

ALVIRA HOTEL

Isaac Newton Langford stepped out onto the porch of the Alvira Hotel and looked out over Lake of Bays. The sun was setting over the forests on the opposite shore, flooding the western sky with a brilliant flash of colour. He had once thought there was no sight more beautiful than the sun setting over Lake of Bays; but now that blood-like crimson glow reminded him of killed dreams. The tourist season had just ended, and the last of the year's guests — a party of hunters from the United States — had left. The hotel was deathly quiet for the first time in months, allowing Langford to ponder his future. Far off, a crow cawed, and Isaac smiled sadly. He felt hollow, dispirited, defeated. A few years before he had thought a bright future lay ahead for him in Dorset, but no longer. How had things gotten to the point where he was actively considering selling the resort into which he had invested so much time, money, and energy? A cloud of unfathomable grief engulfed him as his mind travelled back through the years to the beginning.

Located on the southeast shore of Lake of Bays, in the farthest reaches of Muskoka, the village of Dorset occupies a somewhat isolated location. As one could probably imagine, a century ago, when roads were nothing more than primitive tracks hacked through the wilderness, the community was even more isolated. As a result, Dorset was never really visited by the summer resort craze that swept Muskoka after the 1870s.

Certainly, this wasn't a statement about the area's natural attraction, for the region is home to some of the most ruggedly beautiful terrain anywhere in Muskoka, and the waters are as clear and enticing as any other. The lack of tourism was in large part due to the difficulties involved in getting to Dorset. Nonetheless, a handful of hotels were built in town around the turn of the century, catering to a small tourist population, lumbermen working along the Hollow River watershed, and travellers along the Bobcaygeon Colonization Road (what is today Highway 121).[1] One of the most noteworthy of these resorts was Langford's Alvira Hotel, an establishment that flourished for a time by embracing Dorset's frontier-town atmosphere and selling itself as a sportsman's paradise.

Little is known about Isaac Newton Langford, as he was never well-known enough to inspire the use of much newspaper ink. He was born in London, Ontario, the son and namesake of Irish immigrant Isaac Langford. As a youth, he probably worked on the family farm and dreamt of gaining wealth in a manner that freed him of backbreaking labour. He

The Alvira Hotel was conveniently located near Dorset's wharf.

came to Muskoka around the same time as his brother, George Edward Langford, who would later represent the region in the Legislative Assembly of Ontario, so it's probable that they came together and then went their own ways in search of opportunity.[2]

Isaac arrived in the logging boomtown of Dorset in the late 1880s. The village he found was rough and rustic, a true frontier community consisting of just a handful of homes. Well removed from the heart of Muskoka, Dorset's development lagged far behind other communities in the district. But the village was clearly growing, driven by an influx of land-hungry settlers who believed they could farm the area and, more importantly, by lumbermen working the dense, untapped forests in the region.

Within just a few years, Dorset had grown to include stores, taverns, a school, a church, one small sawmill, and the offices and warehouses of several lumber companies harvesting logs along the Hollow River.[3]

Almost immediately upon arriving, and driven by aspirations of becoming a "self-made man," Langford opened a mercantile on the site currently occupied by Clayton's General Store. He then began campaigning for the lucrative and prestigious postal contract. His efforts were not in vain, and on January 2, 1891, he was named postmaster for Dorset. For a decade or so, Langford seemed content. He was relatively affluent and, as both storekeeper and postmaster, enjoyed a respected position at the heart of Dorset's social scene. By around 1900, however, he began to envision greater things for himself. His thoughts turned to opening a hotel.

At the time, Muskoka was one of the most popular tourist destinations in Canada. Resorts and hotels dotted the attractive lakes, and many owners became extremely wealthy, seemingly overnight. The demand was such that resorts couldn't be built or expanded fast enough to keep pace. Langford saw the potential in the hospitality industry and wanted desperately to be a part of it. But even he must have recognized that it was a gamble to build a resort in Dorset.

First, there was the matter of isolation. Just getting there meant a train ride to Huntsville, followed by a brief trip aboard a steamer across Fairy Lake and Peninsula Lake. Then guests would have to disembark and take a wagon (later a train — the famed Portage Railway) across to Lake of Bays, followed by another few hours on a second steamboat. Would anyone be willing to make that journey?

And would people consider Dorset a worthy destination? It was still a frontier village, after all, and while by the turn of the century most of the rough edges had been filed off with the gradual demise of the logging industry, it wasn't unusual to find coarse and drunken lumberjacks bursting out of tavern doors and onto the village streets.

Langford seemed undeterred. Perhaps he knew that the days of logging in the area were numbered, or that the region's natural beauty more than compensated for any lack of refinement in the community. In any event, around 1900, Langford commissioned local carpenter Charles Drake to build his dream hotel. It was erected on a convenient spot looking out onto the wharf from which passengers would disembark from the steamship, every one of them full of excitement at the prospect of a week or more in the "wilds of Canada."

When looking at early photographs, one is struck by the fact that the Alvira Hotel — named after Longford's beloved wife, Eunice Alvira Langford (née Barker) — is right in the centre of the village. Most resorts of the day were located in natural surroundings, and hence removed from the local community. In many ways, therefore, guests of the Alvira Hotel became guests of Dorset as a whole, and relationships naturally developed between seasonal and year-round residents.

Though the clientele was privileged, in general they were far less wealthy than those who visited the resorts on the other Muskoka Lakes, and as a result the Alvira Hotel wasn't notably grand in either form or furnishings, and its service was not exactly five-star. Nevertheless, the three-storey hotel Drake built was impressive, and the second-largest building in Dorset, dwarfed only by its archrival, the neighbouring Iroquois Hotel.[4]

The wrap-around covered verandas on each level, the pleasant view of Lake of Bays, and the extensive dining room helped created an attractive yet rustic resort. The Alvira had few of the trappings you'd expect from the standard Muskoka holiday of the period. There was no direct waterfront access, no dance hall, and no golf course. There was no tennis court, no swimming pool, and no private launch for tours of the lake. But what the hotel did have in abundance was the beautiful and untouched wilderness, and a population of villagers who had stayed loyal to the traditional, unassuming, and welcoming lifestyle that made Muskoka so compelling, even then.

The guestrooms at the Alvira paled in comparison to the elegance of some of the more famed resorts, and instead were simply and sparsely furnished, though comfortable and clean. Each room had a bed, dresser, and washstand. Guests had to share bathrooms — one per floor. There were no glass chandeliers or fine china in the dining room, but no one complained because the home-cooked meals were outstanding. It was refreshing for some guests not to have to dress up in elaborate clothes for dinner — though, of course, propriety was insisted upon. Guests at the Alvira spent their days swimming, fishing, or canoeing out on the lake. Bonfires and sing-alongs under the pale light of the moon were popular, and guests would hike up to the hills towering over Dorset for unparalleled views out over the lake. The Alvira was, in short, a less pretentious vacation destination for less pretentious people.

Langford promoted the Alvira as "The Place to Get Strength and Happiness" in his print ads. Not particularly inspiring, perhaps, but it seemed to have worked. The hotel was an almost immediate success and it didn't take long for rooms to fill up with guests. Part of the Alvira's popularity was due to its low rates — never more than three dollars per day, or eighteen dollars per week, which was significantly less than its competitors in the region at the time. Another reason was its longer operating season: the Alvira opened several weeks earlier (typically May 1) and remained open more than two months later than most other Muskoka resorts (closing November 20, after the close of hunting season), making it attractive to sportsmen as well as summer vacationers.[5]

In fact, much of the Alvira's success came as a direct result of its appeal to hunters and anglers. Dorset, surrounded by almost virgin wilderness, even into the twentieth century, was a prime destination for such outdoor endeavours. Many of these sportsmen were so impressed by the pristine beauty of the area and the rustic hotel in which they stayed that they began to return during the summer with their families for leisurely vacations. Before long, women were joining their husbands for late-season hunting trips. Almost comically outfitted in long dresses, frilled blouses, and with elaborate hats balanced atop their heads, they eagerly headed out into the woods to hunt deer. It was an exhilarating adventure for them, a chance to cast off the shackles that society placed upon women of the period and to experience something more exciting than the tea parties, formal dances, and church socials they were accustomed to.

None of this would have been possible had it not been for The Huntsville and Lake of Bays Transportation Company, which, with its growing fleet of steamboats, enabled the tourism industry to take root in Dorset and other villages along the shore of the lake. In addition, the owner of the Navigation Company, Captain George Marsh, boosted area resorts with his tireless promotion of tourism on what he referred to as "his lakes."[6] Captain Marsh distributed travel brochures heralding the

Courtesy of Muskoka Heritage Place.

Guests arrived at Dorset aboard the steamship Iroquois. *This was the last leg of a journey that included a lengthy train ride and time aboard another steamer navigating Peninsula Lake. Date unknown.*

appeal of Lake of Bays and organized familiarization trips with railway passenger agents from the northeast United States, all with the goal of spreading the good word about the region and boosting tourism, therefore increasing passenger service on his vessels. This exposure, which Langford couldn't have afforded or arranged on his own, was a huge benefit to the Alvira Hotel, enabling it to develop a reputation in the United States that other resorts of similar size may have lacked.

The growing renown of the Alvira Hotel meant prosperity for Langford, but it also benefitted the community as a whole. During peak season, the number of staff at the resort swelled and there was always summer employment available for the area youth. Other business owners found that the money the visitors spread around provided a measure of comfort previously unimagined. The steady stream of guests to and from the Alvira (as well as the Iroquois Hotel) meant that steamship service to Dorset became more regular, a real boon to the community in an era when the roads were rock-strewn and primitive at the best of times and virtually impassable for much of the year.

"If you've ever been to a seaport, that's what Dorset was like during the days of the steamship," remembers Norm MacKay, a lifelong resident of Dorset and an active participant in the Dorset Heritage Museum. "People would run down to the docks to see the boat coming in and to help passengers with their luggage, and it would wake up the whole village with its horn. It was an exciting period."[7]

It was a good thing that the Alvira Hotel was a success, because it helped to mask disappointments in Langford's other professional interests. In 1904, for example, he lost the lucrative postal contract when the Liberals came to power in Ottawa. It's widely suggested that there may have been some political plotting at work here, and there may be some truth to that. When the Liberals assumed power, they stripped away many favours that had been granted to Conservatives and awarded them to their own supporters. Langford, as the brother of a former Conservative MPP, was caught up in these political games and paid a heavy price in the form of the village postal contract.

A second devastating loss occurred just a few years later, in 1907, when Langford's general store burned to the ground. The building and all

View of Dorset looking north, with the Alvira Hotel's rival, the Iroquois Hotel,
second on the right. Date unknown.

the stock contained within were destroyed in less than an hour. Emotions
writhed within Langford as he stood before the mound of smouldering
rubble. Each grey tendril rising from the ashes seemed to represent an
opportunity, a dream gone up in smoke. The realization that he'd have
to start all over again saddened Langford: three decades lost, just like
that. Though the store was quickly rebuilt, Langford never truly recovered from the personal anguish and the financial damage the fire caused.
Afterward, he experienced a growing dissatisfaction with his life in Dorset.

In 1911, tired out from the effort of juggling two businesses for
relatively modest gain, Isaac Newton Langford sold his businesses and
moved his family away from Dorset.[8] The Alvira Hotel was purchased
by a group of investors from Buffalo, New York, headed by Janet Persch.
The new owners changed the name to The Ganasayo (sometimes spelled
Ganoseo) Resort, which means "the good house" in the tongue of the
Ojibwe Nation. Perhaps not coincidentally, is also the name of a town in
New York State, not far from Buffalo.

The American investors had deeper pockets than Langford, and used
their resources to promote the Ganasayo endlessly and effectively. "Here,

148

the roar of the pavement and the shadow of the skyscraper soon become but the faintest memories tucked in the farthest corner of the vacation-seekers mind," noted one advertisement of the time. Another pointed out, somewhat less romantically, that "hay fever is unknown in the immediate vicinity of Lake of Bays, that portion of Muskoka where 'The Ganoseyo' is located. Many suffering from this disease get relief at once."

Vacationers and sportsmen continued to seek solace at the hotel for a number of years, but whatever hopes Persch and her consortium had of profiting from their purchase were dashed when the First World War began. The steady stream of guests slowed to a trickle, and once the United States joined the conflict in 1917, dried up completely. The Ganasayo was a casualty of the war; closed for the final two years of fighting, its fortunes never completely revived.

Though the resort reopened in 1919, few summer guests returned, and by the early 1920s the Ganasayo's business was almost entirely supported by fall hunters. For most of the year, the resort stood empty, dark, and silent. It was a far cry from the bustle and excitement of the Alvira's early seasons in operation, and was unsustainable. For most people it was clear that the resort's end was near at hand. When it arrived, the end, like that of so many Muskoka resorts, was a spectacularly memorable one.

On December 3, 1927, a fire broke out in the hotel. The building, comfortable though it may have been, was a firetrap, with the aged timbers, wood-panelled walls, and stored furniture and linens providing ideal fuel. As a result, a few flickering flames — probably caused by an electrical short, though some whispered of arson — quickly took hold and developed into a raging inferno. Fire spread rapidly through the deserted guestrooms and halls, so that within a matter of minutes the building was engulfed in orange flames. Villagers alerted by the billowing smoke and the eerie glow of the creeping flames raced to the scene, but any determination to fight the fire melted away when they arrived at the scene and witnessed the strength of the inferno. It was obvious that there was no hope of saving the Ganasayo, and people watched, dumbfounded, as the building — a village landmark for as long as most could remember — was consumed.

When the fire died and the smoke had cleared, quiet and calm returned to the streets of Dorset. Fire was a fact of life in that era, part

Courtesy of Bruce MacClellan.

The Alvira Hotel was last known as the Ganasayo. This image was taken shortly before the resort burned to the ground in 1927.

of the natural cycle, and most buildings that were destroyed by fire were quickly rebuilt. As a result, the village's population were confident that the Ganasayo would rise again. A few months passed, then a year, then three, but there were no signs that the resort would be given a second life. In fact, there was never any serious consideration of rebuilding the resort. It had been limping along for a number of years, so its owners decided there was no point in wasting any more money on it, and simply walked away. The building remained an ugly scar of charred timbers and grey ash over the winter and throughout the next summer. Residents hoped someone would step forward to revive her. No one did. Eventually, the property was sold and redeveloped. Today, a restaurant stands over its foundations.

In time, memories of the Alvira Hotel, like the ashes of its remains, were scattered to the wind. Isaac Newton Langford undoubtedly would have been sad to hear of its demise, but perhaps, too, in light of the way his dreams had been dashed in Dorset, he would experience a tinge of satisfaction in knowing that no one else would reap the rewards of his labour and vision. The December 1927 fire brought to a close the Langford saga in Dorset — a saga that started with so much promise but ended in bitter disappointment.

SEE FOR YOURSELF

Dorset is a pleasingly historic community, with a number of buildings still standing that guests of the Alvira would have been familiar with, foremost among them the Alvira's rival, the Iroquois Hotel, now the Fiery Grill Restaurant. Sadly, however, there is nothing to see of the Alvira. The Dorset Heritage Museum, which boasts a surprisingly diverse collection for such a small community, has a number of photographs and artifacts in its possession relating to the resort. An hour browsing through the gallery, as well as being highly enjoyable, will provide insight into the history of the community that the Alvira helped define and the role the resorts played in its development.

Chapter 10

ELGIN HOUSE

When Lambert Love first had visions of building a hotel for summer vacationers he could never have imagined that it would be one of the most successful and long-lived resorts in Muskoka. For more than a hundred years, successive generations grew up at the famous Elgin House as families returned year after year to enjoy the northern hospitality. This grand old resort is now gone, but the memory of it remains very much alive.

Lambert Love was born in Richmond Hill, Ontario, in 1855, the son of a simple farmer.[1] He apprenticed as a blacksmith for a number of years, mastering his skills with forge and hammer. In May 1879, he married Maggie Isaac, and a year later the newlyweds moved to Gravenhurst, where Lambert worked as a blacksmith and wagon-maker. Though he was a good smith and his services were in constant demand, pounding metal into shape was gruelling work for meagre gains — Lambert soon grew dissatisfied. He had greater ambitions for himself and his family, and with an eye toward that goal, in 1885 he purchased a piece of lakefront property on Lake Joseph, just north of Port Sandfield, that had once belonged to Prospect House founder Enoch Cox (for more on Cox and Prospect House, see Chapter 7). Lambert and Maggie, with infant son Lambert Elgin wrapped up in their arms, headed for their new home with bright hopes for the future.

Elgin House as it originally appeared after being built by blacksmith Lambert Love.

Cox had earlier cleared the land and planted fields of oats, so Love settled easily into the life of a farmer. He also built a sawmill, which he operated for a number of years.[2] Neither occupation rewarded his efforts as richly as he wanted, so while he was comfortable, Lambert was not yet fully satisfied with his position in life.

He might have been pondering his future when he visited the Chicago World's Fair in 1893 and marvelled at all the fantastic changes taking place across the globe. In particular, he noticed how leisure and travel were becoming increasingly popular, and was inspired by the exhibits showing the latest trends in summer resorts across North America. Opportunities in that field seemed to abound for anyone with a vision and a beautiful location. Lambert knew he had both — the enterprise to succeed and a scenic spot on the picturesque waters of Lake Joseph — and when he returned, he decided that he would open a hotel of his own, outfitted in the newest fashions and boasting the latest in amenities.

It wasn't as if Lambert was new to hosting summer guests. In order to generate additional income, the Loves had long copied other Muskoka families by allowing guests into their home for the summer. And they must have been good hosts, because soon the demand was so great that they were turning people away. "Our own home was spacious and we soon had all the guests for the summer that we cared for properly — yes, we were soon bulging at the seams," said Lambert "Bert" Love Jr. many years later.[3]

It wasn't always a smooth relationship between hosts and guests, however. One day, an exhausted Lambert arrived home after working many hours at the mill, eagerly anticipating the moment when he could sink into a chair and relax. He entered his home, threw off his boots, and entered the parlour. To his disgust and dismay, he found a guest sitting in his favourite arm chair. Though upset, Lambert realized he could not ask a paying guest to move, and elected not to make a scene. Perhaps inconveniences such as this, as well as the lack of privacy that was inevitable when one was sharing one's home with guests, prompted him make the decision to build a hotel that was separate from the family residence.

Lambert began planning his new hotel with barely constrained excitement, supposedly using some of the premier resorts of the Adirondacks in New York State as inspiration. Whether he had actually visited these resorts, or simply familiarized himself with their amenities and character from exhibits at the World's Fair is unknown, but he certainly took what was best about these American wilderness resorts and incorporated them into his own.

"My father had made a list of necessities of a hotel (someone said it was on an empty soap carton). The number one spot went to the kitchen, with the dining room to seat 50 guests a very close second, followed by a sitting room and office, all to be on the main floor," wrote Bert Love years later. "The two bedroom floors to have 12 rooms on each floor, with public washrooms. Perhaps here I should say that for an added convenience to complete these rooms, a commode set was to be furnished in each bedroom."[4]

Love knew exactly what he wanted, and was confident he knew what guests wanted, as well.

In 1895, Lambert sold off part of his two-hundred-acre property to pay for the construction of the hotel, and then secured the services of an experienced local builder named Winters. Because he was not a man of half measures, and the building he planned was so ambitious in its scope, it took several years to complete. In the meantime, to create additional funds and continue building a reputation for fine hospitality, Love built five lakeside cottages which he rented out to summer guests. He made sure to lavish attention on vacationers, knowing that if he did so, word of mouth would build demand for his new resort before it even opened. It wasn't until 1898 that the hotel, which Lambert named Elgin House in honour of his son, was finally open for business. It had been a long time in coming, but no one would deny that the wait was worth it: Elgin House was one of the most attractive and luxurious that existed anywhere in Muskoka at that time.

When it opened, Elgin House could accommodate about fifty guests in first-class comfort and with the latest amenities. The grounds were arguably the most beautiful in Muskoka, with manicured lawns, a groomed garden brimming with colourful flowers, and walkways that wound their way through the grounds and into the shaded woods nearby. For recreation there were badminton courts, a lawn-bowling green, beautiful sandy beaches along two miles of shoreline, and a boat livery where canoes and rowboats could be rented. Lambert wasn't one to rest on his laurels and be satisfied with his achievements.

Elgin House after its first round of expansion.

It wasn't merely the first-rate amenities that allowed Elgin House to stand out. Lambert, more so than most of Muskoka's resort owners, realized the importance of excellence in service when it came to the hospitality industry. He had a strict rule of maintaining one staff member for every four guests, which guaranteed that one's needs were always attended to. He also insisted on cleanliness of the buildings and grounds. "When he was at the World's Fair, Lambert Sr. was impressed with how clean the grounds were and how carefully this cleaning was attended to each morning," noted Paul Love, one of Lambert's sons, in an article that appeared in the *Muskoka Sun* many years later. "As a result, the first job each morning for the bellhops at Elgin House was to clean up the grounds."[5]

In an area where farmers struggled, owing to the poor quality of the soil, Elgin House represented welcome jobs for young men and women. Teenage girls were in particular demand as waitresses, housecleaners, and kitchen staff, and as Bert Love later recounted, there was no shortage of candidates. "The neighbours were very anxious to have their daughters in our kitchen under mother's supervision. Help was very plentiful, all very willing and able but with so little training, if any," he said. "I recall trying to train a very fine girl, an excellent worker, as a waitress. We agreed the family table was the place to begin. We tried and tried without success to break her of the habit of smiling sweetly as she served the dessert and asking, '[Is] there any more I can do for you?'" She was polite to a fault, but unable to grasp that, unlike a guest in one's own home, there could be no seconds, and dinner service ended with the serving of dessert. In time, however, these humble farm girls became skilled, professional staff who helped to establish the resort's reputation for excellent service. Few would have been out of place in even the finest of hotels or restaurants.

Elgin House was strictly a teetotalling resort, one of the few that didn't serve alcohol. In keeping with Victorian views toward virtue and frivolity, guests could not play cards, smoke, or even dance. No revealing bathing costumes were allowed; if a woman chose to swim, she had to do so in full dress. Elgin House was considered a very "proper" place. That did not stop the guests from coming, however, and soon it was a well-established place with visitors who returned year after year. Many of these guests were "people of fashion," which meant that they were wealthy.

In those early days, life in the hotel was by today's embellished standards of comfort, quite simple. A hotel back then was distinguished for its "good plain tables" and the accommodations as "good and quiet." For these guests, it was about the peace and quiet that they found in the North, a place to get away and experience all the wonders of Nature.

In 1906, a private two-hundred-seat chapel was built by the staunchly Methodist Love for use by family, staff, and guests. Typically, the chapel was full every Sunday. This, and the rigid restrictions on behaviour, led some to suggest that Elgin House catered to a religious crowd and that guests were required to attend church services. This wasn't the case at all. While most guests were, in fact, Christian, and religion did play a far greater role in their lives than it does to the average person today, the resort made no attempt to force guests to embrace religion. Attendance at Sunday services was purely optional.

Love was full of plans and ambitions, so he saw that half of his salary each year went back into the hotel to make improvements that would ensure Elgin House remained at the forefront of Muskoka's hospitality industry (when Bert was made a full partner, his contract stipulated that he, too, must contribute half his salary to hotel infrastructure). It was rare for a year to go by without some change to the property. Over the years, these improvements included a new and more attractive wharf to ensure that the first and last impressions of the guests were particularly favourable, an eighteen-hole golf course carved from the rugged beauty of the Canadian Shield, electric lighting and steam heat when they were still novelties in Muskoka, and a power plant with a steam-powered generator to provide electricity for lighting and to run the laundry room.[6]

It pained Love to turn away guests, so to keep up with demand, new accommodations were frequently added. In 1910, a new four-storey building with twenty-two additional rooms was erected on the site of the former barn, followed by a new 130-foot-long wing two years later, which housed a pair of expansive, elegant dining rooms to feed the ever-increasing population of summer guests.

Yet, despite constant expansions, a reputation for fine hospitality, and world-class amenities, Elgin House always existed in the shadow of Prospect House, in nearby Port Sandfield. There wasn't any animosity between Lambert Love and Prospect House owner Enoch Cox — indeed, they seemed to get along fine — but there was a rivalry, nonetheless. They were competing for guests, after all, and as proud owners both men wanted their respective resorts to be the finest in the area. Prospect House always seemed to remain on top, dominating the resort scene in Port Sandfield, at least until 1916. On October 15, 1916, the competition ended when Prospect House burned to the ground. It was never rebuilt, ceding its position as the leading hotel in the area to Elgin House. It wasn't how Love wanted to win, but he made sure that Elgin House took advantage of the opportunity to prosper as never before.

By this time, Elgin House, along with a few other resorts, were in a class of their own, offering accommodations and amenities far above those offered by the smaller guest houses around Muskoka. Through the 1920s, Elgin House could comfortably accommodate three hundred guests, the second most of any resort on the Muskoka Lakes — the Royal Muskoka could accommodate more. Rates were $2.50 per day or sixteen dollars per week.

But while the 1920s were a period of prosperity for Elgin House, it was also one of transition. Bert had long been groomed to take over the resort, and with that in mind, he had been made a full partner sometime before 1920. But up until this stage, and despite advancing age, Lambert Sr. never seemed ready to fully hand over the reins to his son. It wasn't that he doubted Bert's ability; he just didn't envision himself retiring. Of course, time pushes relentlessly onward despite our wishes, and by 1925, seventy-year-old Lambert Sr. could no longer deny that he was getting too old to handle the demands of running the resort. Elgin House passed to the next generation of Loves. Incredibly, even as an aged man, Lambert Sr. didn't remain out of the resort business for long, and in 1939 he built a new hotel, which he named Glen Home, for his new wife, Alice — a woman almost half his age — and the two sons that resulted from this second marriage, Paul and John.[7]

Back at Elgin House, Bert proved he had every bit of his father's business savvy and vision, working tirelessly to keep Elgin House up-to-date and, through tireless promotion, among the leading resorts in Canada. In fact, where many Muskoka resorts suffered terribly during the Great

Depression of the 1930s, Bert managed to not only retain his clientele but actually to expand operations. His ability to market the resort to wealthy professionals who may no longer have been able to afford an annual vacation to Europe, but were certainly comfortable enough for a few weeks in Muskoka, guaranteed that Elgin House was rarely less than fully booked, even during the darkest years. During the 1930s, the North Lodge with additional rooms was built, bringing the number of guests Elgin House could accommodate to four hundred.

It's noteworthy that almost all additions to Elgin House, such as the North Lodge and others built by Lambert in the years prior, were separate lodges rather than wings. This was intentional, so that, should a fire break out, the entire resort wouldn't be at risk. As it happens, Elgin House never experienced a serious fire, one of the few Muskoka resorts so blessed. There were, however, two relatively small blazes in the resort's history. One broke out in the kitchen and did considerable damage to the room before it was brought under control. Afterward, while surveying the scope of the destruction, the Loves remembered that they had a whole storehouse full of eggs near at hand that could have been used to put out the flames before it took hold and caused any damage.

Another time, a fire took hold near the four-storey main tower. The alarm was quickly raised and guests hastily evacuated the building by the fastest route possible. All managed to get out safely and efficiently, except for four women who were staying in the tower who, instead of using the fire-escape ropes to slide down to safety, insensibly decided to pack their clothes into their heavy travel trunks and try to manhandle them down the stairs. Halfway down they became stuck, one trunk wedged in the stairwell ahead and another blocking the way back up. Thankfully, the fire was contained and all ended well, but had the staff been slower to react or the fire spread more quickly, all four likely would have died and marred the Elgin House story.

While Bert was clearly an able businessman, the one thing he lacked was the warm, caring, and personable nature of his father. Bert tended to be detached and distant; some, including half-brother Paul Love, have gone so far as to call him cranky. But who could blame him for being a bit distant at times? While Bert Love did come from a privileged world, and many guests considered his resort an idyllic retreat, he was not immune to personal tragedy. Indeed, he endured more than his fair share.

An infant son, for example, drowned in the same waters guests gazed lovingly out at. Later, his beloved wife Mabel died as a result of complications while giving birth to their fifth son, leaving Lambert Elgin almost inconsolable. He never really recovered from her death. The demands of the business and fatherhood forced him to move on, but often the sight of happy families enjoying their time at Elgin House would bring back the memories, and his loneliness would return in a fresh surge. It's likely these melancholy moments were responsible for Bert developing a reputation among some guests for being "dour." And, as if he hadn't suffered enough, another son, Howard, was killed while serving overseas in the Second World War, and in 1947, his father, then ninety years old, passed away.

Bert may have occasionally been distracted, but it had little effect on Elgin House. The glue that held the hotel together was the patronage of guests who returned every season. Staff came and went, even ownership would eventually pass from one individual to the next, but the guests always remained the same. They kept coming back, year after year, generation after generation, providing continuity and a character unique to the hotel. This allowed Elgin House to survive through rough periods — such as the Depression — that caused so many other resorts to fail. Most of the other summer hotels had disappeared by the 1950s, but Elgin House was still going, stronger than ever, its reputation for fine hospitality and warmth intact.

John Bird, who worked at Elgin House throughout this period, remembered what it was like to be a part of this tradition:

> In 1947, I first came to Elgin House as a bellhop. I worked for the Love family then and remember them as good employers. I remember unloading the *Segwun* when it docked, and hoisting dozens of trunks and packing cases on a wagon to be brought up to the hotel.

Like many of the finer Muskoka resorts, Elgin House had a golf course, and both men and women would spend countless hours in good-natured competition.

> [I] and another lad then had to carry everything up to
> the rooms and unpack each [case]. It was just like being
> on an ocean liner, where the steward would hang up all
> those fancy evening gowns and dress clothes.[8]

Guests may have dined and slept in luxury, but for the hard-working, predominantly teenage staff conditions were distinctly more spartan. After a day of catering to the every whim of the paying guests, days which often lasted more than ten hours, a staff member would wearily retire to the isolated staff quarters for a healthy but simple meal and a few hours of down time. Accommodations in the staff quarters, which formerly housed a cheese factory, were pretty basic. Mary Chenhall, who was enrolled at the University of Toronto and waitressed at Elgin House in 1928, remembers the primitive conditions in which she lived that summer:

> The lovely, clear waters of Lake Joseph were our main
> means of cleansing. There was no shower or tub.... We
> had a pitcher and wash basin in our four-by-four room.
> We had to go down to the end of the hall to fill our pitcher

from the single coldwater faucet set in a cubbyhole in the wall. There was a single toilet for the twenty waitresses on the second floor. Consequently, a daily swim was a must. Our hours to swim from the dock were specified so that we would not be interfering with the guests.[9]

There was no recreation room where waitresses could meet and relax, so we had to devise our own entertainment. Lacking much excitement in our lives (and much of the time too tired to enjoy it had it appeared) twelve of us decided to sleep outside on the golf course [one night]. In those days we had no sleeping bags [and] we made a very strange procession as we quietly filed out in our pajamas, carrying a pillow and assorted blankets because it was near the end of the summer and the nights were cool.... We were almost asleep when I opened my eyes for one last look at the myriad stars and was amazed to see several falling stars. Then there were more. I woke Bliss and then the others. As we watched, more and more appeared. There were falling stars everywhere. And then we looked to the north and saw the most amazing display of northern lights that I have ever seen....We had very little sleep that night due more to the heavenly display than to the discomfort of the lumpy ground and the heavy morning dew.

Bliss Pugsley, who also worked as a waitress that summer and was a lifelong friend of Mary Chenhall, recalled that strict restrictions on the waitresses did little to dampen the natural enthusiasm of teenagers away from home, often for the first time: "We swam in the lake's refreshing waters, sneaking a dive now and then off the top of the *Sagamo* docked in front of the hotel, and even once skinny-dipped by the light of the midnight moon. Port Sandfield to Elgin House was a challenging swim for some of us, too."[10]

Time passes on, and by the 1950s Victor Love, Bert's son, had taken over operations. It wasn't just business as usual, however. Victor put his own stamp on Elgin House and made important and long-overdue changes. Most notably, and in keeping with the evolution of societal mores, he lifted the stringent rules against smoking and playing cards. He also tore down some of the older and less well-maintained buildings and removed the top storey and one wing of the main lodge, cutting the number of guests that could be accommodated to a more manageable two hundred. At the same time, he added a dining hall that reflected the tastes of the post-war period, installed a large swimming pool, and built a lakeshore boathouse to hold the resort's fleet of canoes and skiffs.

Victor managed Elgin House for two decades, but in the late 1960s the face of the resort industry started to move away from the beloved Elgin House tradition. Many older guests who had come to the resort each summer and who formed the core of the clientele began to die, but were not being replaced as readily as in former years. The newer generation wanted a vacation experience far different than that which the Loves had taken pride in delivering for almost a century. They wanted a livelier atmosphere, more excitement, and more liberal rules. An aging Victor realized that his antiquated views were out of place with the modern crowd, and in 1971 he sold Elgin House to a gentleman by the name of Didace Grise.[11]

The dining room at Elgin House, circa 1950.

Under Grise's ownership the resort began to attract a younger and far more liberal crowd, but what remained the same was the passion that the employees felt for the historic resort. Perhaps, as the building aged and other resorts of its kind became rarer, the bond between employee and building became even stronger. Cathy Tait certainly felt it. Tait served as the resort's operations manager from 1989–91, and even today feels a particular bond with the property:

> I was resident manager, supervised the bars, handled the purchasing and all the hiring, and scheduled the recreational programming. I guess I did just about everything. Elgin House at the time was the largest resort in Ontario for bus tours, with six busloads of guests arriving every four days for their standard three-night/four-day stays. Almost all would be arriving from the States. What seemed to attract the vacationers was the allure of Muskoka's forests and lakes, which even then were famous across North America, and most especially the scheduled programming that Elgin House had to offer, ensuring the days were full of fun things to do.[12]

Elgin House maintained a large recreational staff to look after the activities and ensure that guests were never without options with which to fill their days. There was live theatre held in the dining room, water sports, tennis lessons, dance lessons, games nights, and a wide variety of sports to try one's hand at — everything from archery to shuffleboard. This programming was a huge draw for vacationers, though if one's idea of a vacation was to quietly curl up on a chair overlooking the lake that was certainly an option.

Great food was another draw. Over the decades, Elgin House developed a fine reputation for its menus. As Cathy Tait recalls:

> We had three food outlets, each one with a different feel. There was the dining room, main lodge, and the most

popular, the lakeside Deck Lounge. This was an outside terrace where people could enjoy a meal or simply a few drinks on beautiful summer days. The Deck Lounge was open to visitors as well as guests, and because it was located along the water, many cottagers came over by boat. It was a real hot spot on the lake. Even at [that time] people ... dressed up for dinner, probably because a lot of our guests were older people who were raised with the tradition of wearing formal jackets and dresses for dinner. It was a charming throwback to another era, and staff loved it.... I know I did.

Rooms were plain and rustic but no one seamed to care because people were so busy that they were only in the rooms at night to sleep. The prices were very affordable at only $99 per night, all-inclusive.

Throughout the 1980s, Elgin House remained consistently full and profitable. Before they left, many guests would book for the next summer and even put a deposit down. In light of this, no one could have predicted that the end of this magnificent hotel was near at hand. When the end came, it was sudden, traumatic, and completely unexpected.

"Financial mismanagement caused the resort to go bankrupt in 1991, not lack of business or some unfortunate incident, like the fires that destroyed a lot of Muskoka resorts. The resort was successful right until the end, with about ninety percent occupancy at all times," said Cathy Tait, who found the hotel's demise particularly painful. In fact, business was so good that the owners wanted to expand to keep up with the demand and to add new amenities. To finance the changes they took another mortgage. It was a gamble, and it failed terribly. At the time the economy was strong and Elgin House was valued at $15 million. A few years later, the economy fell out from underfoot, and the resort was devalued to a mere $2 million. Suddenly, the owners couldn't make the mortgage payments and, despite desperate attempts to right the sinking ship, Elgin House drowned under a swell of rising debt.

"The resort went into receivership and closed, and the contents were sold off in an auction. Thousands ... of people wanted a piece of that resort because it was so historic," remembers Tait. "I couldn't watch it happen, so I went down to Toronto for the weekend. On my way back there was a lineup of cars and trucks on Highway 400 carrying antique chairs, beds, and tables. Anything that could be picked up was sold, even fixtures like faucets and banisters. The place was raped, and I couldn't help but compare these people to vultures. When I returned, the buildings were empty … nothing like the buildings I had come to know so well. You wouldn't recognize them. It was heartbreaking to watch because I was so fond of the place."

Cathy remained on the property at the request of the receivers, who asked her to watch for vandals and be alert for fire. Alone on 450 acres, she watched with a heavy heart as the buildings fell apart and the grounds became overgrown. "It was kind of like the movie *The Shining*," she says, laughing. "The grass was four feet tall and bears had moved in it. It was just me and my dog out there, and it was kind of creepy."

By 1993, Cathy knew it was time to move on. But the property was too beautiful, too ideally situated to remain unused for long, and so it surprised no one when the land was purchased for development two years later. The buyer was the ClubLink Corporation, Canada's largest owner, operator, and developer of high-quality golf courses and resort properties. Little time was wasted in tearing down the sad, weathered old buildings and redesigning the property as the exclusive Lake Joseph Club Resort, featuring modern cottages, a popular water-accessible restaurant, and an eighteen-hole golf course that was promptly named the Best New Golf Course in Canada by both *Golf Digest* and *SCOREGolf* magazines in 1997.

A renewed excitement and energy may have returned, but for many, nothing can replace the century-old tradition that was Elgin House. The resort, as with so many other similar resorts that once graced Muskoka, can now only live in the memories of those who visited it. It was particularly saddening for us to write this chapter, to listen as people reminisced, and to look at pictures of this grand old place, knowing that we will never experience it for ourselves. It would have been an honour to have been able to walk through its front doors and enjoy a peaceful vacation as people had for a hundred years. A grand tradition is now gone from Muskoka.

SEE FOR YOURSELF

Little remains of Elgin House today. The century-old chapel remains and is designated as a historic building. It is occasionally used during weddings held at Lake Joseph Club Resort. The Grise residence is still standing, as well, and is now used as an office. Renowned golf-course architect Thomas McBroom made use of some of Elgin House's historic golf course while designing the resort's modern twenty-seven-hole course. And guests staying at the resort or eating at the Water's Edge restaurant enjoy the same stunningly scenic views of Lake Joseph as guests of Elgin House did all those years ago.

Chapter 11

. . . .

PAIGNTON HOUSE

The scenic property graced today by the magnificent J.W. Marriott Rosseau Resort and Spa in Minett has been attracting vacationers since John Frederick Pain opened his farmhouse to hunters and anglers back in the 1880s. As any modern guest would attest to, the views out onto Lake Rosseau are memorable, the waters refreshingly cool, and the encompassing wilderness wraps the property in a hushed shroud ideal for relaxation. Ask any developer and he'll tell you this property is among the finest in Muskoka.

With such enticing natural splendour, it was only a matter of time before someone decided to build a summer resort. But when J.F. Pain established Paignton House, he did far more than just build a hotel. He also laid the foundation for a family legacy that would see four successive generations invest their hearts and souls in the resort, each one further enhancing Paignton House's reputation as the premier family-friendly summer destination in Muskoka. "Family Run for Family Fun" wasn't merely an advertising slogan, but rather a guiding principle the Pains lived by.

It's been forty years since Paignton House left the family, since Archie Pain made the heart-rending decision to sell the hotel that his grandfather had founded and in which he himself had invested so much passion and toil. It's been a decade since the historic inn was replaced by a modern luxury resort. Still, the passage of years hasn't dulled the vivid memories Archie's children have of growing up and working at Paignton House, nor has it made it easier for them to accept that the historic resort is gone. It's clear that the story of Paignton House isn't really one of a summer hotel and its countless anonymous guests, but rather one of a family who, over a century, imbedded their very spirit into the property.

As such, we must start with the 1845 birth of John Frederick Pain in Calcutta, India. Pain's father was a wealthy Englishman who, as a shipmaster and merchant, made a small fortune trading between Asia and Europe during the 1840s and '50s. The elder Pain also had interests in West Africa, where he had a partnership in a lucrative palm oil business.

Young J.F. lived in India for part of his youth, and at some point contracted malaria. He would suffer from its effects throughout his life. In fact, it's been suggested that the chronic effects of the illness were directly responsible for Pain's arrival in Muskoka. His parents, so the story goes, listened to the advice of a physician and shipped their eleven-year-old son to Canada in 1866 with the belief that Muskoka's fresh air and invigorating climate would restore his fragile constitution. His nagging symptoms were indeed largely alleviated, but J.F. remained a weak, lethargic man throughout his life.

That's just one possible explanation for how John Frederick Pain arrived in Muskoka. There are others. One theory put forward was that he was a troublesome young man and was sent to Canada by is father to make something of himself, or perhaps to distance him from some scandal. If J.F. did commit some terrible act that marred the family reputation and compelled his parents to put an ocean's distance between them and their son, it's gone unrecorded and is best categorized as mere folklore.

A third theory says Pain came to Muskoka under the auspices of the Wrenshall brothers, Frederick and William, who came in 1866 and began clearing land for a farm.[1] The Wrenshalls apparently had an ingenious way of obtaining free labour to assist them in fulfilling the requirements as laid out by the Homesteads Act: they would place advertisements in British papers to lure the sons of rich Englishmen into the wilds, promising a hands-on education in the skills necessary to become a successful homesteader. The Wrenshalls would get free labour, and their young wards would gain valuable experience that they could later put to use by claiming lots in their own names. Since the Wrenshalls had very limited experience in Muskoka, this arrangement was something of a scam, but if the stories are to be believed, it worked well enough to attract at least one young lad: J.F. Pain.

Whatever circumstances led John to Muskoka, he arrived in 1866. He spent the winter of 1866 with the Wrenshall brothers on Royal Muskoka Island, but by 1867 was homesteading on his own. He first settled on land at a place called The Bluff, near Juddhaven, located on the western shore of Lake Rosseau, but soon moved to another site nearby — later the home of a small summer resort called Thorel House.[2] This land, according to the scrupulously particular Pain, was too open and windy, and so he moved for a third time, in 1869. He finally settled on a property near the hamlet of Minett, in a sheltered bay on Lake Rosseau, with a sandy beach and spectacular views.

It was a magnificent parcel of land worthy of his privileged background. But for the first few years, at least, Pain lived more like a pauper than a prince. "The first thing homesteaders did was cut down the trees and plant potatoes and turnips around the roots of the trees. The rotting leaves made for good soil. I think the vitamin E in the turnips kept them alive. It was thick virgin forest and deer were scarce back then, but I'm sure the fishing was good," explained Archie Pain years later as he reflected back on his grandfather's life. "The closest supply was Washago for sugar or flour. Now they've been known to snowshoe to Washago to bring back supplies on a toboggan. My dad used to walk to Bracebridge. He'd go down one day and come back the next. It must have taken three or four days to go to Washago and back."[3]

Things were tough, especially for a man who was far from hardy and who had little experience with manual labour. J.F.'s one great success in these early years was his marriage to Charlotte Tuck, a good, solid woman who was unafraid of hard work and had a wealth of practical experience. John had become acquainted with his neighbour Michael Woods, a fellow homesteader who would one day build a resort known as Woodington House.[4] The two men assisted each other with laborious tasks, as pioneers frequently did, and soon became close friends. One day, J.F. paid his neighbour a visit and was pleased to find another visitor in the Woods home, Michael's sister-in-law, Charlotte. Pretty and like-able, J.F. was smitten. He began to actively pursue her, and eventually he succeeded to gaining her hand in marriage.

While no doubt Michael and Martha Woods considered the wealthy, educated, and cultured Pain a suitable husband, in truth it was John who benefited most from the union. According to his descendants, J.F. had "never really learned how to farm," and wasn't really the working type.[5] "He was a gentleman who always wore a vest and tie. His wife milked the cows and did the work," recalled Archie Pain.[6]

Between doing her household chores and rearing three kids — Fred, Nell, and Richard "Dick" Dickinson — Charlotte found the time and energy to ensure that the farm provided enough for the family to eat. Her workload only increased when the Pains began to take fishermen and hunters into their home for a few evenings at a time, offering accommodations and a hearty meal in exchange for a few dollars.

Like many settlers in the area, the Pains discovered how difficult it was to transform the dense wilderness into fields of grain and to grow vegetables in the barren soil. There had to be a better way to make a living. When they saw how well sportsmen would pay for their hospitality, and when these same sportsmen began to return with their families to enjoy the refreshing beauty of Muskoka, many farmers began to transform their homes into summer hotels. The Pains were actually slower than most in taking that leap. It wasn't until the mid-1890s, when they saw the great success of nearby Clevelands House, that J.F. and Charlotte began seriously considering their options. In the end, they decided to follow the trend and enter the hospitality industry.

Throughout 1894 the Pain home underwent renovations that saw it expand into a small resort capable of accommodating fifty guests in comfortable, but hardly luxurious, fashion. J.F. named it Paignton House, after a town in England in which his family had lived for a time during his youth. No longer would the family share their home with guests; a separate house was built nearby.

With the demand for summer accommodations so great, Paignton House had little trouble attracting guests in its inaugural 1895 season, and it wasn't long before its reputation was rivalling that of nearby

Clevelands House. Once again, much of the credit must go to Charlotte Pain. While J.F. was the face of the hotel, a sociable fellow who spent much of his day entertaining guests, his wife quietly worked behind the scenes to make sure everything functioned smoothly. The resort's reputation hinged to a great degree on its excellent food, which was the result of the countless hours she spent unseen by guests in a stifling kitchen, expertly preparing their meals. She was tireless, and instrumental in Paignton House's success. So while John Frederick Pain is credited with founding one of Muskoka's most enduring resorts, much of the credit must really go to his wife.

Over the decades that followed, thousands of guests would enjoy Paignton House's hospitality and were captivated by its charm. The resort grew both in size and reputation. In 1911, for example, seven additional guest rooms were added the lodge, along with a larger, more modern dining room and a welcoming lobby. Plans for further additions were interrupted by the outbreak of the First World War in 1914. Consecutive years of dismal business seemed to tire J.F., and his passion for the resort waned. In 1918, just as the war was entering its bloody finale, the seventy-three-year-old decided to retire and pass the torch to his son, Dick.

Dick was, in many ways, the polar opposite of his father. Whereas the elder Pain shunned hard work, Dick was unafraid of manual labour, and actually seemed to revel in it. In that regard, he was more like his mother. Also like his mother, he was practical and driven by common sense, qualities that would help him navigate some tough times at the helm of the family resort. Where J.F. and Dick were similar was in their spirit of enterprise: both men wanted to taste success, to make a name for themselves, to build an enviable reputation for the hotel.

When Dick took over Paignton House, it had sat empty for a number of years. The building and grounds needed revitalization, but more so, its customer base had to be revived because it had been out of the public mind for so long. Other resorts were expanding and becoming more refined, and Paignton House had to adapt or risk falling behind. Dick, assisted by his wife Marie (née MacNaughton), was determined to restore the resort to its pre-war success, if not surpass it. It would be a huge and costly job, but they were young and energetic.

Dick began confidently, selling some land along the shore of Lake Rosseau to finance the construction of a third-storey addition to the lodge, which would allow Paignton House to comfortably handle one hundred guests. While this would still make Paignton House only a mid-sized resort by the definition of the day, it represented the most significant growth in the resort's twenty-year history. As it turned out, even after the expansion doubled the capacity, there still weren't enough guest rooms to go around. Either paying customers would have to be turned away, which any hotel proprietor would naturally be reluctant to do, or more accommodations had to be added. Predictably, Dick chose the latter and, during the 1920s, began building a number of guest cabins. At the same time, a new and much larger steamer wharf was added to make for a more favourable first impression and to allow the increased number of guests to come and go in a timely fashion. Amenities such as tennis courts and a lawn-bowling green were also added.

To help finance these constant additions and to supplement the family income, each winter Dick packed his bags and headed north to Cobalt to toil in the silver mines. Having seen the lean years of the First World War, Dick sensibly lavished attention on the family farm, as well. More acreage was put under cultivation and the amount of livestock increased. This meant that the resort was almost entirely self-sufficient in terms of poultry, meat, milk, and vegetables. It also ensured that the family had something to sustain them when the Depression arrived, nearly sinking the tourism industry in Muskoka.

While his energy seemed to be boundless, every man has his limits. Luckily, Dick was blessed with three sons — John, Robert, and Archie — to help around the resort and farm, and in whom he instilled a matchless work ethic.

Even as youngsters, there were always chores to be done. "I had to go and milk the cows ... sometimes I'd have to find them first. They could be two miles away," Archie later recounted. He'd also carry trunks up to guest rooms, cut firewood (the resort burned thirty cords of split wood in the cookstove each summer), maintain the grounds, and guide people to Bruce Lake, with its plentiful stock of fish. "My biggest source of income," Archie hastily added, "was picking dew worms at night after a rain, which I sold to tourists for one cent each."[7]

As Archie matured into a young man, his jobs also came to include piloting the resort's thirty-six-foot boat, the *Minerva*, in which he took guests on sightseeing cruises of the lake and to the golf and country club at Port Carling. Mostly, though, he took passengers to the Royal Muskoka for a night of dancing, with music performed by the legends of the Big Band Era, such as Tommy Dorsey and Louis Armstrong: "I'd take a load down to the dance halls and would dance every night ... one night there were 2,200 people there [at the Royal Muskoka]. They were spilling out onto the lawns. They couldn't seat them all ... it would be just bouncing. Lit up at night, it was a beautiful hotel."[8]

The Depression proved to be a tough period in Paignton House's history, but it weathered the turbulence better than many of its contemporaries. One of the reasons for its relative good fortune was the decision to serve alcohol on the premises, a decision that was only reached after long consideration, and even then only reluctantly by a very conservative Dick Pain. Most Muskoka resorts were dry at the time, partly due to the lingering effects of prohibition, but largely because they retained the Victorian values that prevailed decades earlier when they were established. Archie, seeing the vibrancy that partying brought to the Royal Muskoka, was convinced that Paignton House should tap into that energy, as well. "It took me two years to talk Dad into it. It was the first tavern in Muskoka in 1937, selling beer. A cocktail licence came years later," Archie recalled. "We did good business. It saved the day, really."[9] When the pub opened, Paignton House became the party headquarters on Lake Rosseau, a lively place where drinking, dancing, and carousing were the order of the day. It profited from the fact it was for many years the only hotel on the western side of the lake with a liquor licence. The good times had returned.

Fate intervened in the form of another world war. Unlike during the First World War, the resort did not see its business completely evaporate, but the atmosphere certainly took on a more sombre tone. It wasn't easy to frolic in the lake, relax under a shady tree, or share a joyous drink while men were dying overseas. For the Pain family, the war was highly personal because Archie enlisted in the army and spent years overseas.

Paignton House, circa 1939.

They continued to put on a brave face and smile for guests — life goes on, after all — but they didn't feel much like celebrating. Thankfully, Archie returned safely at war's end, and life quickly returned to normal.

Changes were afoot at Paignton House, however. In 1946, Archie wed Betty Cope, a woman from Port Carling whom he had met while home on leave two years earlier.[10] The two of them, along with Archie's brother John and his wife Agnes, began to take a more active role in operating the resort, with an eye toward eventually succeeding Dick. They learned the details of operating the business — everything from advertising and promotions to cooking for two hundred guests, hiring and training staff, and customer service. It was an apprenticeship that lasted years. Finally, in 1954, fifty-nine-year-old Dick Pain agreed it was time to move on, and he sold Paignton House to his sons. It was around this time that the resort shifted its focus again, now catering largely to family groups.

With families firmly in mind, Paignton House boasted one of the more developed children's programs of any resort on the lakes. Parents would drop their kids off at 9:30 in the morning and pick them up for lunch, then return them at 2:00 p.m. and leave them once again until

The lakefront was always a focal point of life at Paignton House, with guests swimming, boating, or simply lounging by the water. Date unknown.

7:00 in the evening. An early dinner was served for the little ones at 5:00 p.m., thus freeing up the parents to enjoy a quiet meal.

Children loved their time at the resort, and spent joyful days doing arts and crafts, swimming, hiking, and playing games. The resort even offered a full-day trip to Santa's Village in Bracebridge for the little ones. There can be little doubt that the first-rate children's program was an integral part of Paignton House's popularity throughout the post-war period. Adults had their own share of exciting activities to occupy their days, including swimming, canoeing, boating, shuffleboard, tennis, golf, and horseback riding. In addition, the Red Wing Flying Service would come on a weekly basis to take guests up in a floatplane for an aerial tour of Lake Rosseau, and the *Lady Elgin* would regularly come by to take people for leisurely scenic cruises. In the evenings, guests would enjoy campfires, sing-alongs, dancing in the Hyde-a-Way Lounge, and live entertainment. There was something for everyone, and never a dull moment.

While Archie and Robert were equal partners, it was Archie and Betty, and their five children — Susan, Peggy, Ann-Marie, Janet, and Doug — who lived on the premises and ran the resort. Archie handled

177

Everyone loved swimming off the Paignton House dock. Photo circa 1950s.

all the maintenance and renovations, and even the construction of the golf course. He also took an active role in preparing lunches and dinners. "Dad would handle the cooking of omelets at lunch and would do all the meat-carving at dinner. He also did all the barbeques, masterfully grilling over two hundred steaks on an old clawfoot bathtub filled with charcoal [and] topped with a homemade grate that he put together with a frame and a double layer of chicken wire," explains Janet Wallace, Archie's middle daughter.[11]

Betty, for her part, began in the office, performing administrative tasks, but by the 1960s was full-time in the kitchen. As Janet recalls:

> She worked herself ragged in temperatures over a hundred degrees on a cool day, and you never heard a single complaint from her lips. When the weather was particularly hot, she would get up before her usual 5:30 a.m. and go up to the kitchen to prepare special salads for

the staff to enjoy. She always looked after her family and in the summer her family included all the staff. There were over forty staff members [who] lived at the resort, so she was a busy mom!

Paignton House was a true family-run operation, with the Pain children taking an active and important role from a very young age, and it was not uncommon for them to miss school because they were needed at home to work. "There was never a time that I remember not contributing to the running of the hotel. Even as very young kids we would pick rocks off the ground and put them on a stoneboat when Dad was creating his golf course. Then I remember that I had the responsibility of placing all the dishes back on the shelves after breakfast and lunch … I would have been eight or nine years old," Janet recalls.

As the children aged, their responsibilities grew. Susan, the eldest, was in charge of reservations and customer service, Ann-Marie worked in the kitchen, Peggy assisted in administrative tasks in the office, and Janet ran the dining room and organized the staff talent night, held weekly in the Hyde-a-Way Lounge. Often, the staff members they supervised were several years older then they were. It was a lot of responsibility for the teenaged Pain children, who learned from a young age how to interact with people and be independent beyond their years.

Even though the resort was only open during the summer months, there was no time off for the family during the winter. That was when mailings went out for the next year to secure new reservations. "Mom would lead the charge, the kids would sit around at the dining-room table, the typewriters would come out, envelopes and wet tongues at the ready, and the process would begin. Every evening the envelopes would be addressed, stuffed with brochures and rate cards, stamped, and piled, ready to be mailed out the next day. I remember well the year we were gifted with a stamp machine and we no longer suffered paper cuts on our lips and tongues," says Janet. Winter was also a busy period for doing maintenance work, which seemed to take up an increasing amount of time as the buildings aged.

While most of the seasonal staff were teenagers, Archie had a soft spot for the underdog and turned the hotel into an opportunity for

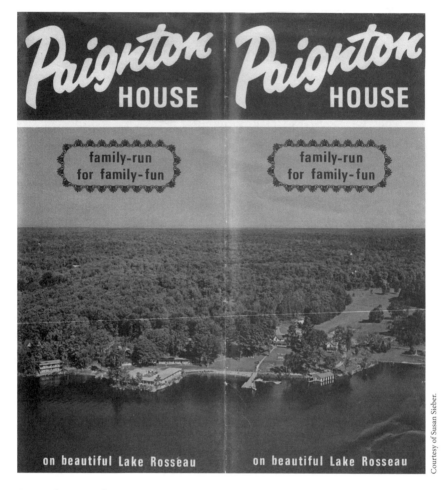

Poster dating to the 1960s. Paignton House had always had a reputation as a family-friendly resort, but the philosophy was really embraced by the owners in the post-war period, when they offered children's programming that was the envy of any Muskoka resort.

men battling alcoholism to get a second chance and put their lives in order. Generally, these men would be chefs who had a skill set difficult for any summer resort to acquire due to their seasonal nature. Archie recognized their potential value and would go down to Toronto to pick them up, set them up in a room, and then would nurse them through the alcohol withdrawal. They, in turn, would reward him with hard work and loyalty throughout the summer. In fact, many so respected Archie that they would leave their money in Dad's charge to be sent to them on a monthly basis during the winter so that they would not lose it all in drunken binges once they returned to Toronto in the fall.

As in the case of any substance abuser, it was difficult for these individuals to shake their dependency. As a result, Archie's decision to employ alcoholic chefs meant there were occasional adventures in the Paignton House kitchen, as Janet explains:

> There was an old abandoned car out in the bush and on the rare occasion that "the thirst" would win the battle, they would disappear for a couple of days and live in the car, drinking themselves sick. After a couple more days, they would return to their place in the kitchen as of nothing was amiss. During their time away, Dad would step into their place in the kitchen. Those men were a part of our family and stayed with us for over a decade.

In 1968, Archie bought out his brother and became sole owner of Paignton House. Five years later, he decided to sell the resort to Ken Fowler, a developer with more than forty restaurant and bar venues to his name, including the Fairmont Hot Springs Resort in British Columbia. "My father sold for health reasons," explains Doug Pain, Archie's son, who today lives beside the Rosseau Resort on the Pain's original land grant from the 1860s. "It wasn't that he was ill, but he was seventy-three years old and, as he aged, things stressed him a lot more. He was just too old to be running the resort anymore, and the offer from Ken Fowler was too good to pass up. He deserved the rest, and had a long, happy retirement as a result."

Paignton House was a blend of the familiar and the new during the 1970s. On the one hand, the resort retained its well-deserved reputation as one of the most family-friendly resorts in Muskoka, and a sense of continuity was retained by the hiring of Susan Pain and her first husband, Don Vincent, to manage the resort. On the other hand, there was a refreshing sense of excitement as new developments sprang up on the property, most notably a pair of two-storey buildings housing additional guest rooms. At the same time, a former Royal Navy steam launch, the *Nottingham Castle*, was purchased to serve as a yacht for guests. Fowler had ambitious plans for Paignton House.

"The resort was one of the nicer ones in Muskoka, the property was extremely attractive, and the Pain family had run it well. There was a lot of potential there," remembers Ken Fowler, who fell in love with the region while attending a summer camp on the shores of Kahshe Lake as a teenager.[12] "But we wanted to bring it into the 1970s. We made a number of additions, all with an eye toward updating the facilities and moving toward a four-season resort, which we knew was the way forward. We were one of the few resorts who attempted to open year-round. The summer business remained family-oriented, while in the winter we moved toward couples and conferences."

Unfortunately, Fowler was blocked in his efforts to really develop it as the luxurious, multi-faceted resort that he envisioned and which he instinctively knew would be a success. "We didn't see an opportunity to grow it because there was a lack of zoning and services, and because there seemed to be little enthusiasm from local government," Fowler says, explaining his decision to sell in 1987.

In the ensuing years, Paignton House changed hands a couple of times, and by 1993 was in receivership. Meanwhile, Fowler saw opportunity in the District of Muskoka's new official plan and bought back the property with a view toward implementing his dream of building a major resort. To make that happen, he began by acquiring neighbouring properties, eventually accumulating 1,384 acres, including Clevelands House Resort and one mile of lakefront. But he moved slowly in implementing his grand scheme and held off on major construction until a fire in 2000 forced his hand.

Paignton House had been blessed to have gone more than a century without fire, but its string of good fortune came to a sudden end on June 29, 2000. The resort was not yet in full summer swing, but a number of guest rooms were occupied at the time with several dozen youthful summer employees who were on hand getting things ready for the flood of guests that would soon swamp the hotel. Around 1:00 a.m., co-owner Dermot O'Carroll was awakened from a sound sleep by a panicked staff member. All grogginess disappeared the minute he heard the dreaded word — *fire*. O'Carroll raced to the scene, fearful of what he would find. To his mild surprise, the fire was relatively small and seemed contained to one area. Rather than call the fire department, he decided to organize his employees to fight the flames themselves. "It was a very minor fire at the time. We had buckets of water, hoses, every fire extinguisher we could grab in the hotel," he recounted for local reporters just after the fire.[13] It was a fateful decision, and the delay in contacting the fire department would have disastrous repercussions.

What began as a small fire had, despite their efforts at containment and elimination, slowly but steadily spread. By 1:45 it was obvious that the blaze was beyond their ability to handle it and a call went out to the fire department. Twenty minutes later, the Minett volunteer firefighters arrived on scene, led by Station Chief Winston Gonneau who, ironically, had worked at Paignton House as a teenager in the 1950s. He immediately recognized that more men were needed, because by now the flames were spreading rapidly and burning extremely hot. Additional firemen from Port Carling and Bala joined the fight. By then, a wall of orange-red flames was racing from room to room within the building, consuming everything in its path. Firefighters who had bravely entered the building had to beat a hasty retreat when the roof above began to groan ominously. Only minutes after they vacated the building, the roof gave one final pained groan and then collapsed. Paignton House was lost. All that remained to be done was to ensure that the flames did not spread.

By 7:00 a.m. the fire had been extinguished, reducing the once-charming hotel to a clapboard shell of black, smouldering ruins. O'Carroll was stunned. While the owners had actually planned to demolish the old building in the fall and replace it with a more modern four-season resort, they were still counting on the revenue from that summer's guests. Now the season was over before it had even begun, the result, it was later determined, of a faulty electric heater. Perhaps more upsetting to long-time residents of the area was the fact that nothing of Paignton House could now be preserved. Instead, the building was unceremoniously torn down that fall. "They smashed it to pieces. They smashed the stainless steel fridges, [and] the late-model expensive doors and windows," said Archie Pain, who was understandably upset by the destruction of the building that contained so many family memories.

What replaced Paignton House was the Rosseau Resort and Spa, a world-class property that was partnered with J.W. Marriott Hotels in order to bring it international recognition. The $120-million development features an indoor/outdoor pool, a luxuriant spa and hair salon, two restaurants, a ballroom, and a challenging golf course, The Rock, designed by Nick Faldo. "We envisioned a high-quality tourist destination, but also wanted to retain the feeling of a classic Muskoka resort. The Royal Muskoka Hotel, at one time probably the largest and most magnificent resort in Muskoka, was located just up the road, and we incorporated some of its character into The Rosseau. When you're inside the resort, you feel a connection to the Muskoka resorts of old. That was intentional," explains Fowler.

The all-season resort was intended to be the centrepiece of the ambitious Red Leaves Project, a $700-million project that would include a resort village complete with town square, stores, cafes, restaurants, art galleries, and a boardwalk along almost one and a quarter miles of Lake Rosseau shoreline. While plans for the village soon stalled, the Rosseau Resort and Spa quickly gained a reputation as arguably the finest hotel in Muskoka. Feasting at the fine-dining restaurants, luxuriating in the spa, exploring the beautifully landscaped grounds, or admiring the stunning views over the lake … in every respect, The Rosseau Resort and Spa is magical.

But one can't help but miss Paignton House, with his rich history and its family-atmosphere. It's not just the Pain family that looks back nostalgically at the lost resort. Pamela Patchet spent many happy summers at the resort as a child, and recounted her memories in an article in *The Muskokan* years later. She provided the hotel with a touching epitaph: "Paignton House is long gone. It is now the site of the majestic Red Leaves, but sometimes, if I concentrate, I can almost smell the pines and hear that brass bell ringing through the woods announcing one more dinner."[14]

That's the effect Paignton House has on anyone who knew and loved it; years may pass, but cherished memories of enchanted summers spent there remain oh so vivid.

SEE FOR YOURSELF

The opulence and majesty of the Rosseau Resort and Spa overshadows the few reminders of Paignton House that still exist. From the terrace of the main building, looking down toward Lake Rosseau, you can see the battered remains of one historic building. This wasn't part of Paignton House proper, but rather was a private cottage used by the Pain family. Even though they lived just a short distance away, on the other side of the resort, come summertime they would migrate to the cottage, just as city people would have done. The building has seen better years, but dates to the 1890s or very early 1900s. To the left of the cottage is Fish Rock, which, graced with Muskoka chairs and jutting out onto the lake, is a beautiful place to watch the sunset. Guests have been enjoying the scenic spot for as long as anyone can remember, and it one of the few parts of the property that wasn't altered when the Red Leaves development began.

View of Fish Rock from the Paignton House pier. Fish Rock remains a beautiful spot beloved by guests of the Rosseau Resort and Spa. Date unknown.

Chapter 12

·······································

WINDERMERE HOUSE

When one thinks of Muskoka's historic resorts, the iconic image of Windermere House — white siding and twin turrets on a gentle slope above Lake Rosseau — almost inevitably comes to mind. It's the resort which best honours its glorious heritage while also embracing the needs and pleasures of modern tourists. It's the Muskoka hotel you go to if you want to connect with summer vacationers of a century ago; strolling around the grounds in the fresh lakeside air or lounging in the luxuriant comforts of the building itself, the experience feels so nostalgic that it's easy to forget that the Windermere House of today is merely a faithful reconstruction of the original, fire-ravaged property. Rich in history, even richer in class, many would argue that Windermere House isn't just a resort but a symbol of Muskoka and its tradition of hospitality.

Thomas Aitken was twenty-eight years old when he arrived in Muskoka in 1860,[1] lured by the much-advertised free land being given away under the Free Grants and Homestead Act. When he claimed his two-hundred-acre bush lot in Watt Township, he couldn't possibly know that he would one day found a Muskoka icon, a summer hotel that came to epitomize the best qualities of a wilderness resort. At the time of his arrival, all he wanted was a fresh start. Clearing the forested land and turning it into a

An early photo with a historical curiosity: note the sign for "Maple Leaf Hotel"
beside the buggy, circa 1910.

farm represented a task in which he could lose himself in order to forget
the grief that hounded him. Just a year prior, Aitken's beloved wife, Janet,
had died in childbirth along with the baby she carried. Fleeing his suffering, the young widower left Scotland and headed for Canada, accompanied by two cousins, his sister Ellen, and her husband, David Fife.[2]

They settled first at Rice Lake, in Otonabee Township (Peterborough
County), but since most of the best land in the vicinity was already taken,
Thomas, along with David and Ellen, pushed on and headed for the free
lands of Muskoka. The wound of having lost his wife was still fresh and
painful when they arrived at their lots and, axe in hand, began the task
of taming the wilderness. As it was with any homesteader, one of the first
chores that Aitken faced was that of building a log shanty; the primitive log cabin he built that autumn served as his home for a decade, and
stood near where the fourth green of the Windermere Golf Course is
located today.

Our knowledge of Aitken's first years in Muskoka is fragmentary,
and some sources even suggest he may have spent some years working
on Great Lake steamers. But he must have devoted considerable energy
to his homestead, because Seymour Penson, a contemporary observer

who kept a detailed diary, noted that "they [Aitken and the Fifes] were industrious, and well on their way to prosperity."

Around this time, David Fife encouraged his brother-in-law to move closer to the lakeshore, and even allowed him to build a new home on his property. Aitken agreed, and erected a more refined home on a slight rise overlooking Lake Rosseau, a home that became the local post office in 1870 when he took on the job of postmaster.

The post office had previously been run out of Archibald Taylor's sawmill. Taylor, a native of the Lake District in England, named the post office Windermere after a picturesque lake in his home region. One day, he simply dumped the mailbag on Aitken's porch and said he'd had enough. Aitken accepted the job, and when he did, the name Windermere moved to his property. The rest, as they say, is history.

In 1872, Thomas Aitken took a new wife, Mary Traill, a widow with two children, John and Mary, from her previous marriage. Around this time, he discovered he could make money taking guests into his home for a few nights at a time. He certainly wasn't alone; all around the Muskoka Lakes, settlers disillusioned with the meagre gains of their farmland were finding they had more success in the hospitality industry and were taking the first tentative steps in that direction. But if Aitken hadn't been married, he couldn't have possibly juggled a farm, the chores associated with being the village postmaster, and the operation of a summer boarding house. Though she gets short shrift in history books, Mary deserves much of the credit for Windermere's success in its early years. It was she who did the cooking and cleaning for guests, and, in contrast to Thomas's taciturn personality, she was more friendly and hospitable.

At the time, guests amounted to a handful of fishermen each year, demanding little more in the way of comforts than a roof over their heads and a few square meals. And that's all they got; Windermere House circa 1872 was a far cry from the luxury resort of today. When guests arrived, Aitken and his family gave up their beds and moved into a woodshed, vacating their home for a couple of nights in exchange for a few dollars. "Straw ticks were used for mattresses, with wheat straw being saved for this purpose. Each day, the straw in the ticks had to be fluffed, and when it became broken, was discarded and replaced with fresh," remembers

Matthew Fife in the Fife family history, *Down Memory Lane*. "No springs or mattresses were in use in these days. The straw ticks were placed directly on the bed slats."

One of the early guests taken with Windermere, even in its first rustic years when it was little more than a boarding house, was Timothy Eaton of department store fame.[3] Eaton came to love the area so much that he built his own cottage, Ravenscrag, within view of Windermere, and it was reputedly he who encouraged Aitken to wholeheartedly embrace the tourist industry and develop a true summer hotel.

Aitken was swayed by Eaton's arguments and in 1874 began to make improvements to his home with an eye toward turning it into a real resort. Sadly, Mary didn't live to see the work completed; she had delivered a healthy son, William, in 1873, but tragically died giving birth to a daughter, Minnie, three years later. Thomas was now forced to raise two young children, two stepchildren, and manage an expanding tourist business on his own.

Somehow he more than got by, because by 1883 the resort was so successful that a huge new addition — including Windermere's first tower — was built in order to meet demand. At the same time, Thomas finally bought the land upon which Windermere House had been sitting from David Fife. For the sum of forty dollars he received the 4.6 acres bounded by Windermere Road and Golf and Fife Avenues. That same year, as if to celebrate his achievements, the fifty-one-year-old Aitken married Elizabeth Boyer. The couple would have two children: daughter Gertrude was born in 1888, followed by a son, Leslie, in 1889.

By 1887, Windermere House had begun to look like the resort we know today, with a three-storey wing facing the lake, intersecting with a three-storey wing facing Windermere Road. Thomas's original home, overshadowed by the new additions, was still being used to accommodate guests.

Thomas and Elizabeth (who earned the nickname Queen Victoria for her imperious ways) were very strict with the locally hired staff, setting down a firm set of rules that had to be followed. Staff members weren't allowed to befriend guests, for example, and couldn't even speak to them unless it was in the course of performing their duties. Staff were required at all times to present a strictly professional demeanor, and laughing and the outward expression of joy were frowned upon. Finally, card playing, the consumption of alcohol, and smoking were forbidden.

Thomas and Elizabeth also demanded hard work and maintained high expectations in terms of cleanliness. The painted grey floors, for example, had to be washed by hand every day in what was a painstaking process that left knees and backs aching. "They washed them [the floors] with water and soap, and when that dried they mopped them with skim milk. When it dried it made the floor shiny," remembers Mary McPherson, whose mother, Sarah Earnshaw, worked at Windermere House in the 1890s.[4]

Windermere House's success is all the more incredible when one considers the personality of Thomas Aitken. Unlike so many of the more successful hotel proprietors of the day, Aitken was neither outgoing nor personable, and seemed almost reluctant to serve as the jovial host. Seymour Penson went so far as to consider him "dark and taciturn," suggesting a moodiness that would have been out of place in such a welcoming inn. Still, he was certainly doing something right, because Windermere House's reputation continued to grow. Doctor John Potts, a guest in 1886, noted that, "it is a quiet, respectable house, just the place for families needing rest and the best of air."[5] Quiet and respectable probably best describe Aitken, as well.

By the 1890s, prices had risen from $7 to $10.50 per week (with special rates for families), reflecting the growth in comfort, services, and amenities. The hotel could accommodate 220 guests, who spent their leisure hours in quiet pursuits such as croquet, tennis, or lawn bowling, or engaged in a game of checkers or dominoes. Boating was popular, as well, since the beautiful waters of Lake Rosseau were one of the chief attractions that lured tourists to Muskoka. In keeping with etiquette appropriate to the upper-class society to whom the resort catered, "drinking parties, carousing, and objectionable noise" were forbidden.

Continued demand meant that Thomas was not yet finished adding to Windermere House. In the winter of 1902–03, Thomas expanded the front wing of the hotel, adding the second tower and additional accommodations. At the same time he added acetylene lighting, which lasted

Windermere House, Lake Rosseau, Muskoka, Canada.

Courtesy of Muskoka Lakes Museum.

An early colour postcard, dating to the early 1900s.

until the village was hooked up with hydroelectricity in 1930. He also built a concrete water tower to provide the hotel with a consistent supply of water for plumbing and washing. This tower still stands today, in a grove of trees behind the resort. The last notable change during Thomas's lifetime was the sale in 1919 of a portion of the original two-hundred-acre Aitken land grant to the newly formed Windermere Golf and Country Club. Parting with the land may have been somewhat sorrowful for Thomas, but he knew it was a wise decision, as the addition of a golf course would make Windermere infinitely more attractive to wealthy summer visitors.

Unfortunately, signing the papers to conclude the sale was one of the last acts Thomas Aitken would perform. He died later that year, on December 23, 1919. He was an old man who had lived a remarkably full life, rising from a humble background to establish one of Muskoka's iconic resorts. Thomas passed away just as Windermere was entering its most prosperous era yet, and it was his children, Leslie and Gertrude, who took over the hotel and proudly watched as it bloomed during the exciting 1920s. (Thomas's first-born, William, wanted nothing to do with Windermere and contented himself with running the village store.)

Courtesy of Muskoka Lakes Museum.

Windermere House, circa 1903. Under magnification, one can see by the different shaded shingles where Thomas Aitken added on to the original building.

Elizabeth Aitken remained in the picture, as well, a grey-haired, grandmotherly figure who could often be found socializing with long-time guests or simply sitting in her favourite chair on the veranda looking out over the lake.

Gertrude Aitken married a man named Charlie Roper and the couple lived in the Aitkens' early home, located near the Anglican church. Uncomfortable in the spotlight, Gertrude looked after the housekeeping at Windermere and managed the mostly female staff. By this time, Windermere was particularly popular with guests from Ohio, New York, and Pennsylvania, and many of these American guests were now arriving in chauffeur-driven luxury automobiles. Gertrude's husband, Charlie, managed the garage, which provided fuel, service, and indoor storage for guests' vehicles.

While Gertrude and Charlie provided essential services without which the resort could not have operated, it was Leslie and his wife, Maude Dakar, who were largely responsible for the excitement and invigorated reputation that propelled Windermere to new heights during the 1920s.

Maude, originally from Cleveland, Ohio, had come to Windermere as a guest with her family in 1914. There she met and fell in love with her future husband. The passion that bloomed turned into a passion for the resort that had brought them together; Windermere began to take on a most romantic atmosphere. The decor was upgraded to give a veneer of elegance, and many argued that its rooms were now more beautifully outfitted than those at the celebrated Royal Muskoka Hotel. Leslie and Maude also hired an orchestra that played gentle music during dinner and switched to dance music as the night wore on. Guests always dressed for dinner, with the men in suits and ties and the women in long, beautiful gowns. "Windermere was a genteel kind of place," said Shirley Martin, whose family spent entire summers at Windermere House in the 1920s and '30s.[6] Gid Rowntree, a young cottager at the time, was equally impressed: "I thought if I went in, they'd throw me out. It had a certain high-class ambience."[7]

It wasn't just the ambience that evolved during this period. Windermere's physical appearance changed, as well. The Aitkens added a sunroom and beauty parlour to appeal to the high-class guests, who increasingly demanded greater luxuries and services and more refined hospitality. Mrs. Timothy Eaton, wife of the millionaire founder of Eaton's Department Store, was a frequent client of the parlour and was well-known for being demanding and impatient. Fearing her wrath, the stylists would be certain not to book anyone before her so as to guarantee she wouldn't have to wait.

While these additions were being made, the two-storey wooden veranda that had characterized the resort from the very beginning had deteriorated and now threatened to drop off the side of the building. It had to be removed. Replacing it was a unique and attractive stone veranda. By this time, Windermere had taken on its now familiar appearance: twin towers, sparkling white siding, candy-striped awnings, and a welcoming porch with a view of the lake.

Mrs. Eaton wasn't the only famous guest at this time. Perhaps the most famous wasn't a businessman or a wealthy socialite, but rather World War One flying ace and hero William "Billy" Bishop. He spent many summers at Windermere, flying up by float plane and offering guests scenic flights over Muskoka. For a time, he had even operated an air passenger service that brought guests to Muskoka in record time — an hour or two from Toronto as opposed to the better part of a day. It seemed like a great idea, but such a venture was ahead of its time and folded after a few short years. Bishop struck up an enduring friendship with Charlie Roper, who similarly had a passion for aviation. It was said that he would hop into a plane with the same ease as you or I would get behind the wheel of a car. He was reluctant to take guests up, however.

Shortly after the end of the Second World War, extensive renovations on the first and second floors of the hotel reduced the number of rooms but created larger suites and allowed private bathrooms to be installed for the first time. The renovations were so extensive that they amounted to virtually constructing a new building inside the old one. Floors and walls were rebuilt, as settling had so warped them over the years that flat surfaces were almost non-existent, and new wiring and plumbing was installed throughout. It was costly and time-consuming, but an up-to-date Windermere that was better able to survive in the modern world emerged. During the course of the work an 1883 edition of *The Northern Advocate* newspaper was found nailed to the wall in one of the dormers, obviously placed there to show the year that part of the hotel had been built.

Mary Elizabeth Aitken, the daughter of Leslie and Maude, had been trained from a young age to succeed her parents and operate the resort. Sadly, nothing could have prepared her for the suddenness by which the transition took place. Her mother died in 1950 and her father just two years later, plunging the thirty-one-year-old into the depths of the hotel management business, a responsibility she knew one day would be hers but that she never imagined would come so soon. Her Aunt Gertrude and Uncle Charlie helped out, as always, but the responsibility for the success or failure of Windermere House was hers alone. To her credit, Mary Elizabeth, a strong-willed and independent woman, succeeded in shaping the resort so that it remained relevant and a popular Muskoka destination in spite of changing trends in the tourism industry.

Under her guidance, the resort gained a reputation for fine dining. The secret to her success was a deal she struck with the University of

Toronto's Hart House, by which she was allowed to hire their chefs for the summer when Hart House was closed. These chefs, masters trained in Europe with skills that rivalled those in any fine dining establishment, brought a sense of refinement and indulgence to the dining room. As a result, Friday and Saturday dinner services at Windermere House would often seat four hundred people.

Mary Elizabeth also recognized that diners would like to enjoy a glass of wine with their meal and so arranged for a liquor licence in 1971. When word of this got out, people in the village of Windermere were enraged. Their tiny community had remained dry even while the municipalities around it had long since allowed the sale of alcohol. It must have hurt Mary Elizabeth to discover that the person leading the opposition was her uncle, Charlie Roper. Some villagers never set foot in the building again and some guests refused to return, but most people recognized the liquor licence to be a sound business decision that allowed Windermere to better compete with other resorts and restaurants in Muskoka.

Other prominent changes under Mary Elizabeth's time as owner included the opening of the Bird Cage Room, where people could dance and enjoy an after-dinner drink, and the Settler's Bay development, composed of self-contained all-season units built on the site of the former Fife House.

Even as other historic resorts in Muskoka were closing, Windermere continued to thrive. Mary Elizabeth had every right to be proud of her success. Yet there is a touch of sadness to her story. She never married, so had no one with which to celebrate her achievements. In 1975 she was diagnosed with cancer, and while the disease went into remission after a lengthy battle, Mary Elizabeth decided to remove herself from the stress of running a resort. Sadly, the cancer was lying dormant, but not defeated, and it returned a few years later, along with two tumors. Mary Elizabeth died on April 10, 1987, just shy of her sixty-sixth birthday.

The end of the Aitken years marked the beginning of a decade-long period of instability for Windermere House, as a succession of owners came and went. By this point the building was more than one hundred years old, and it was showing its age. Considerable money would need to be invested to repair, renovate, and modernize the resort. A series of

Windermere's white walls, candy-cane awnings, and twin towers are the best-known features of this Muskoka icon.

owners, each with good intentions, took over management of Windermere House, only to be defeated by the scope of the challenge. In one year alone, the septic system gave out and had to be replaced and the walls of the swimming pool collapsed, necessitating the construction of a new pool.

In 1985, Windermere House underwent a three-million-dollar facelift, but the work was mostly cosmetic in nature. So while the property presented a pretty face to the public, serious underlying problems remained. Every spring the building shifted, leading to slanted floors and warped doors. When the water was turned on in April, there were invariably half a dozen leaks in the pipes that had to be patched. When it rained, water would seep into the building and collect in bubbles behind the wallpaper. During severe thunderstorms, water would rise so high in the basement washroom that it could be heard sloshing back and forth against the door. The cost of upkeep, let alone modernizing Windermere House to keep it up-to-date with what the paying pubic expected of an elegant resort, was quite prohibitive. As could have been predicted, by 1992 the hotel was in receivership, and when there was still no buyer two years later, the receiver let it be known that it would not reopen the hotel for the 1995 season. People throughout Muskoka were under no illusions what that meant; they had seen enough resorts come and go over the years to know that once closed, old buildings deteriorate so rapidly that soon the only option left is to tear them down.

Thankfully, saviours emerged to rescue Windermere House from a tragic demise. Bill Wakefield was a local cottager who was moved by the grand old lady's plight. Something about the resort's past stirred him, and every time he entered he felt as if he were following in history's footsteps. Wakefield knew he had to act to save Windermere House, and so he recruited a group of seventeen investors. Each one had some special tie to the property. Some had vacationed there for years, or had fond memories of working there in their youth. Others had grown up at neighbouring cottages and couldn't imagine Windermere without the imposing white hotel at its centre. At least one couple involved had been married there years earlier.

The new Windermere House Corporation, with Bill Wakefield serving as president, sunk $400,000 into the property just to get it ready for the 1995 season. Their efforts did not go unrecognized by a grateful community, and that year they were awarded the Built Heritage Award from the Muskoka Heritage Foundation for preserving what was widely held to be a regional treasure.

In the autumn of 1995, Hollywood location managers arrived in Muskoka and began to search for an old-style hotel to serve as the setting for an action film, *The Long Kiss Goodnight*, starring Geena Davis and Samuel L. Jackson. The filmmakers had initially settled on Pinelands Resort, but Bruce Reville, the resort owner, suddenly changed his mind and left the crew without a location, with filming only a few months away.

In desperation, they approached the owners of Windermere House for permission to shoot at the resort. After some deliberation, the owners agreed. It would be good exposure for the hotel, the $45,000 location fee would be welcomed, and, since the resort was closed for the winter, there would be no disruption to their usual business. It seemed like a great opportunity, but one owner, Bill Wakefield, seemed to have reservations. Before putting his name to the contract, he reputedly said to the location manager, "If you burn this down, I will tear your heart out." It was an ominous thing to say, almost as if he had a premonition.

It wasn't as if Windermere House was new to show business. In 1985, producer Kevin Sullivan had filmed the exterior for a scene in the movie *Anne of Green Gables*, starring Megan Follows. The resort was supposed to be the fictional White Sands Hotel, and so it seemed only appropriate that many of Windermere's staff filled in as extras in the scene. Windermere House had a starring role in its next film appearance, the movie *Switching Channels*, starring Christopher Reeve, Kathleen Turner, and Burt Reynolds. Once again, many staff members served as extras.

But something was different when it came to *A Long Kiss Goodnight*. Perhaps it was the scale of the movie, or the fact that it was a high-octane, explosive action film. Whatever it was, Wakefield was apprehensive, but allowed the movie to go ahead nonetheless.

Filming began in February 1996. Excitement over the production was high, with residents of the sleepy community enjoying the attention of Hollywood and the opportunity to find winter employment as extras (some two hundred locals were hired, earning as much as three hundred dollars a day). Mindful of their promise to safeguard the property, the filmmakers hired three members of Windermere's volunteer fire department to serve on site twenty-four hours a day. A pump was installed at the lake and a hose was run up to the hotel. With these precautions, and safe in the knowledge that the Windermere fire station was just a mile down the road should the unthinkable happen, the filmmakers assumed they had taken every reasonable safeguard, and turned their attention to shooting the movie.

The evening of February 26 was miserably cold, with freezing rain falling from a black sky. A few hours earlier the sun had been shining brightly and the day had been unseasonably warm, but with the coming of darkness the temperature had dropped like a stone and clouds heavy with rain had rolled in. Cast and crew tugged the hoods of their parkas tighter as they shot a snowmobile chase scene out on the frozen waters of Lake Rosseau. Just after 11:00 p.m., a member of the production team turned from the stinging rain and stepped into the shelter of Windermere House. He climbed the stairs to the second floor, looking for a room in which to hold interviews the next day. He drew up suddenly, the hairs on the back of his neck tingling as he sensed danger. The smell of smoke hung in the air. Wisps of smoke curling out from one of the rooms confirmed his fears: Windermere House was on fire. Panicked, the crewmember raced to raise the alarm.

Firefighters converged on room 226, where a thousand-watt halogen bulb had been set up and directed outside to illuminate the scene. Flames and a dense cloud of smoke greeted them. Reacting quickly, the firefighters were sure they had put out the fire. But flames suddenly erupted in the adjoining room. Moments later, flames burst through the roof near the west tower. The walls of Windermere House were hollow, effectively acting like a chimney, causing the flames to rise out of reach of the desperate firemen. Within minutes, the flames were crawling along the roof's ridge and racing along the hallways of both the second and third floors. Panicked calls went out to all area fire departments, but the roads were virtually impassable due to a sheet of ice that had formed over them, preventing the fire departments from Port Carling, Milford Bay, and Bracebridge from arriving in a timely manner. In truth, there was little they could have done, even if they arrived sooner; the flames simply spread too quickly and burned too hot. The fire raged so hot, in fact, that it disintegrated every porcelain sink and toilet in the building.

As firefighters struggled to contain the inferno, people were evacuated from neighbouring homes and the entire village poured out onto the icy streets. Standing in the cold rain, shivering, many crying, everyone was in a state of disbelief as they observed the chaos around them. Sirens blared in the distance as dozens of movie crewmembers wandered around in a daze, some perhaps feeling in part responsible for the disaster. Smoke rose from the building like a black veil, and flames burned so intensely that the sky turned an eerie red. The effect was clearly visible from as far away as Ufford and Raymond, and from across the lake at Port Carling, where it was assumed that it was some sort of special effects for the film. Taking it all in, many Windermere residents felt anger gradually swelling up. They had entrusted the filmmakers with a community treasure, and that trust had been broken.

"I remember watching the first tower fall and about an hour later the second tower falling and I knew there was no way to save the hotel," recalls Jeff Brown, who worked at Windermere House for over twenty years before retiring in 2010. "I had to call the main shareholders and inform them that the hotel was burning and was down to the main floor. The telephone went dead on the other line for a few minutes as they struggled with their emotions. It was not the most pleasant call I have made. It wasn't until 5:00 the next morning that the fire stopped burning. By this point, the only things remaining were the veranda's stone pillars, though when we sifted through the rubble later we found some menus that survived because they had been encased in ice by the water being poured on the building by firefighters."[8]

Members of the community, and indeed people from across the region, were in deep shock at the loss of the Muskoka icon. During the gloomy days after the blaze, some of the grieving owners debated whether Windermere House should be rebuilt, and if it was, what form the new Windermere House should take. In the end, they believed they had a duty to return the resort to its rightful place and to restore it as faithfully as possible. A "rubble-turning" ceremony was held on July 17, 1996, and work commenced immediately, using photos and historical floor plans to conform as closely as possible to the original design. Windermere House reopened on May 31, 1997, with Premier Mike Harris signing the register as the first official guest. A tradition was restored.

Today, more than a decade later, and with another change of ownership (as of 2010, the resort is owned by Paul Jefferies), Windermere House retains the exterior appearance of the original building, as well as much of its charm, but it now offers the height of comfort and elegance. Guests may now indulge in fine dining at one of three restaurants: the upscale Rosseau Grill, Windermere Pub and Bar, and the Wasabi Sushi Café. They luxuriate in unsurpassed comfort, whether it is in the privacy of their own comfortable rooms or at the Windermere House Spa, a restful retreat that offers massages, facials, pedicures, and manicures. And they can enjoy carefree recreation, ranging from swimming in the heated outdoor pool to casual walks around the quaint village of Windermere or golfing at Windermere Gold Club, the oldest in Muskoka. The resort blends nostalgia with luxury in a seamless package that's unique in the area.

Courtesy of Windermere House.

Windermere House is located at the heart of the historic village of Windermere. Many of the heritage buildings in town have ties to Windermere House and its founding Aitken family.

SEE FOR YOURSELF

Architecturally, Windermere House looks so much like the original that many guests forget that it's an entirely new building, only a decade old. That's part of its charm. But there are direct, if unseen, links to the past. Workers discovered hundreds of square-headed nails that date back to when Windermere House was built. These nails have been hammered back into the new building. In addition, a piece of timber salvaged from the sunroom window has been fashioned into a time capsule that contains a selection of letters, photos, and newspaper clippings from the hotel's past, intended to be opened in 2096, one hundred years after the new Windermere House was built.

For more tangible evidence of the resort's heritage, enjoy a brief walk through the quaint hamlet that surrounds it. Just behind the resort, looming over Christ Church, is a water tower that dates to the 1920s. To the south of Christ Church is the Windermere Cottage, today part of the resort but formerly the home of Thomas Aitken, and then the residence of his daughter Gertrude and her husband Charlie Roper.

Opposite the Windermere Golf and Country Club is a small, rustic cottage that was built in 1921 as the home of Leslie and Maude Aitken. Their daughter, Mary Elizabeth, lived here until her death. Farther on, you come to Windermere United Church, built in 1950, which contains a memorial window commemorating the Aitkens and other families who contributed much to Windermere's development. Finally, on the other side of Windermere Road, just to the south, sits a squat concrete building. This was used as a garage by Charlie Roper to house and service guests' cars, and in later years it became the Windermere House laundry. Today it is used as a maintenance building. All told, this insightful walk through a century of Windermere history takes approximately half an hour.

Chapter 13

MORE MUSKOKA RESORTS

Muskoka had far too many historic resorts to comfortably fit within the confines of one book. In fact, during the course of our research we've identified more than 150, from tiny Pleasant House to the majestic Royal Muskoka Hotel. The wealth of options made narrowing down the field to just twelve a difficult chore, and we inevitably found ourselves having to put aside some that were particularly interesting, because of space constraints. Rather than cut them entirely, however, we elected to include the history of ten of these resorts here, in capsule form, in a final chapter that also serves as a preview to *Muskoka Resorts: Then and Now Volume II*, the intended sequel to this book.

THE BEAUMARIS HOTEL

Beaumaris is a small island in the middle of Lake Muskoka, a speck of green jutting up from the crystalline blue depths of the lake. It's hard to imagine that at one time this unassuming island was home to a resort that challenged for the title of Muskoka's grandest hotel during the first half of the twentieth century.

The story of Beaumaris's brush with fame begins in 1872, when the island was divided in two: Edward Prowse took the southern half, and

John Willmott received the northern. Willmott threw himself into his role as homesteader, but Prowse had greater things in mind. He decided to go into the hotel business, and by 1883 had transformed his house into a three-storey vacation property, which he called the Beaumaris Hotel, after the resort village of Beaumaris, located on Anglesey Island in Britain.

The response from the public was so enthusiastic that additions were soon in order. Only four years after opening, the hotel was catering to 150 guests. To keep patrons entertained, Prowse invested heavily in the latest in amenities, including lawn-tennis courts, a croquet field, dance hall, billiard room, and even a bowling alley. Most of the guests were wealthy Americans; in fact, so many vacationers hailed from Pittsburgh that the Beaumaris soon acquired the nickname "Little Pittsburgh."

Thanks to its popularity as one of the premier tourist destinations among America's elite, the resort continued to grow. By 1906 it could accommodate two hundred guests, and the property boasted an eighteen-hole golf course, the first of its kind in Muskoka.

Edward Prowse died in 1910, but the tradition of excellence in hospitality he had provided was carried on by his son, Horace E. Prowse, until his own retirement in 1919. The resort was then sold to Andrew Nicholson of Toronto, and upon his death in 1923, it passed to his brother George.

The Beaumaris Hotel was still thriving two decades later when fire razed the hotel on the night of July 22, 1945. What makes its fiery demise doubly tragic was the fact that the fire had been deliberately set by a youth employed at the hotel. The resort was filled to capacity at the time, but fortunately the only casualty was the elegant hotel itself. It was never rebuilt.

CHELTONIA HOUSE

Now a part of Clevelands House, Cheltonia House was for almost sixty years a successful summer hotel in its own right. But it's appropriate that the two resorts have merged into one, since there was always an extremely close bond between them. William and Louisa Fraling, who opened

Cheltonia House, were close neighbours of the Minetts of Clevelands House. There was a familial connection, as well, as Louisa was a cousin of Arthur Minett.

Cheltonia House opened in 1910. Louisa almost single-handedly ran the hotel. She did the laundry, the cooking, the housecleaning, the book-keeping, and the marketing. William's sole job, it seemed, was socializing with guests. It didn't take Louisa long to realize this was a one-sided arrangement, so she parted ways with William and ran Cheltonia House on her own. To her credit, she was very successful and guided the hotel through two world wars and the Great Depression. One of the resort's biggest attractions was Louisa's food; she was widely hailed as one of the best cooks in the area. But she kept the secrets of her success close to the vest. If you asked her for a recipe, she'd leave something out so you could never quite replicate it.

As she aged, Louisa's son Evan and his wife Olive took a hand in running the resort. (Evan also ran his own successful general store and boat livery on the property.) Louisa continued to operate the resort well into her eighties, though by then it had been reduced to just a few cottages, a far cry from its heyday, when as many as eighty guests relaxed under the shady trees and anxiously awaited the mouth-watering dinners.

The resort finally closed around 1969. A decade later, in 1980, the fifteen-acre property was purchased by Clevelands House and the historic Cheltonia House was renamed The Manor House, serving as accommodations for guests of the family-oriented resort.

CLEVELANDS HOUSE

In 1867, twenty-five-year-old Charles Minett, an English cabinetmaker from Bishop's Cleeve, set sail for Canada with his young wife, Fanny White. Minett worked his trade in Toronto for a number of years, and might have remained a humble and largely anonymous craftsman had fate not intervened. After contracting a severe case of bronchitis, his physician urged him to move north to the healthful, restorative climate of Muskoka.

Heeding the advice, in 1869 the Minetts packed up their worldly belongings and set off for the harsh, largely uninhabited wilderness.

Charles proved to be a capable farmer and soon became relatively affluent, which allowed him the resources to build a fine two-storey home. With room to spare, the Minetts began to take in summer visitors. According to local lore, among the earliest guests was a pair of English aristocrats, Lord Lambert and Earl Baker, who had travelled to Muskoka to hunt and fish but had gotten stranded in the snow. They ended up remaining with the Minetts for six months, and it was they who encouraged Charles to build a hotel.

Minett took the suggestion to heart and began construction in 1881. The completed hotel was named Clevelands House, named after Cleevelands House, Minett's ancestral home. No one knows how the extra *e* was dropped, but one story says that it was the result of an error made in the printing of the hotel register in 1883. No correction was ever made, and it's been Clevelands House ever since.

The resort did a booming business from the beginning, and by as early as 1887 expansions were undertaken in earnest to keep up with demand. In 1891, Charles began another round of additions that would add a third storey to the hotel. Unfortunately, while construction was underway, he fell and suffered grievous injuries that would in time contribute to his death.

Numerous other changes occurred over the next century as the hotel grew and guests' tastes evolved. One thing that remained the same, however, was the atmosphere: Clevelands House was never intended to be luxurious, but rather homey and family-friendly. Fun, not formality, was the rule of the day. It remains that way today, a pleasing mix of modern and traditional; an ideal vacation spot for families looking for leisure rather than luxury.

THE DELTA SHERWOOD INN

Sherwood Inn opened during the tail end of the era of Muskoka's grand resorts. It reflected the changing tastes of tourists who, by the late 1930s and as a result of the sobering effects of the Great Depression, were increasingly demanding smaller, less opulent accommodations. It remains a popular and historic property seven decades after it first emerged on Muskoka's hospitality scene.

Sherwood Inn was built in 1939 by a Toronto lawyer named Charles Draper as a comfortable, welcoming property full of country charm. It struck a chord with the public, because Sherwood Inn thrived in the decades that followed even as the larger, more famed Muskoka resorts struggled. Over the next half-century, Sherwood Inn was carefully developed by a succession of owners who added modern amenities and touches of class, but always made sure to remain true to the resort's rustic charm. The most notable owners were the Heinnecks, who took over in 1979 and focused on dining excellence. Their efforts paid off a few years later when Sherwood Inn earned the prestigious CAA/AAA Four Diamond Award for outstanding dining service.

Seventy years of tradition went up in smoke on September 18, 2009, when Sherwood Inn, then owned by Delta Hotels and Resorts, was ravaged by fire. Heroic efforts by the staff ensured that no guests were injured, but the historic main lodge was gutted by the flames. Thankfully, Delta Sherwood Inn rose from the ashes a year later, reborn and invigorated, yet still exuding the same rustic charm that had always captured the imagination of its guests.

THE GRANDVIEW INN

The Grandview Inn was the product of the vision and ambition of Minnie Cookson, who despite a humble background would create one of Muskoka's best-known and most enduring resorts. Minnie Pleace came to Canada as a Barnardo child, one of countless orphans who were sent from Britain to live on bush farms and work as labourers for their foster families. Minnie ran away from her placement and was taken in by the kindly Froats family of Huntsville. While there, she met and fell in love with her neighbour, John Cookson, whose family owned an extensive farm along the shores of Fairy Lake.

John was content to be a farmer, but Minnie envisioned a hotel overlooking the picturesque waters, and she convinced her reluctant husband to give her five acres of farmland on which to build an inn. In 1911, the three-storey, twenty-eight-room hotel she called Grandview opened for business. Ads boasted that it was the inn with the million-dollar view. Enticed by these promotions, as well as by Minnie's fine cooking and the reasonable rates, guests began to flock to Fairy Lake. The resort was almost entirely self-sufficient, since the 650-acre farm provided all of its vegetables, milk, berries, chicken, and lamb.

John Cookson died in 1917, but Minnie carried on for twenty more years, until her death in 1937. Her daughter, Rose Cookson, a woman every bit as independent and strong-willed as her mother, took over the management of Grandview Inn and guided it to three decades of success. After Rose's death in 1970, Judy and Bruce Craik purchased the tired, weathered old resort and began extensive renovations that saw it evolve over the next twenty years into a sophisticated resort. The Grandview is today owned by Delta Hotels and Resorts, but it has retained its reputation as one of the oldest and most attractive resorts in Muskoka.

HAMMILL'S HOTEL

Though there were dozens of resorts on Lakes Muskoka and Rosseau, very few existed on their sister lake, Lake Joseph, the most westerly of the three. The largest summer hotel operating on that body of water was Hammill's Hotel, which endured a long but somewhat troubled existence.

Thomas Hammill arrived on the shores of Lake Joseph in the 1870s as a modest settler content to work his land, but by 1886 he was supplementing his income by guiding sportsmen to the best fishing and hunting spots in the area, and by renting boats to them. The next logical step was to house and feed them on his farm, and by 1890 his home was being advertised as Hammill's Hotel. In addition to ready access to prime fishing and hunting locales, the hotel also boasted a fine sandy beach and complete serenity in its secluded bay. As a result, families as well as sportsmen began to frequent Hammill's, necessitating a series of expansions. By 1909, as many as one hundred guests could be accommodated.

By this peak period, however, Thomas Hammill was no longer operating the hotel. Instead, it was in the capable hands of his son and daughter-in-law. They, in turn, sold it to J.D. Williams a few years later, and then it passed to Reverend L.S.D. Croxon.

Croxon's era as proprietor was marked by sadness and tragedy. The Depression undermined the hotel's fortunes, so that it sat empty for years on end and left the reverend grieving for the resort he had grown to love. His grief came to a sudden and tragic end in 1934. The reverend was aboard the steamship *Waome* when it suddenly sank, and he drowned in the waters of Lake Muskoka.

Hammill's Hotel became the Lantern Inn under new ownership, but no change of name could restore its former vitality. In 1946, the dilapidated and forlorn old building was torn down and a cottage built on top of its stone foundation.

LIMBERLOST LODGE

Limberlost Lodge defined the concept of the wilderness getaway; it was as if the term "getting back to nature" was created to describe a stay at this resort located deep in the midst of virgin forests on the border of Algonquin Park. It was built in 1921 by Gordon Hill as a haven for those with a passion for outdoor sports, boasting more than two hundred miles of trails for hiking, cross-country skiing, and horseback riding. "The charm of the Limberlost country, deep in the forest," suggested an early promotional pamphlet, "is the maze of small lakes and streams, rocky wooded ridges, deserted clearings, saddle trails, and old pioneer roads ..."

Limberlost was unique among Muskoka's resorts of the time because it was open year-round, and came to develop a particularly fine reputation for its winter sporting activities. In 1934, an 1,800-foot-long alpine ski hill known as The Top of the World was developed (the peak may not have been the top of the world, but it certainly was the top of Muskoka, as Limberlost occupies the highest elevation in the region). With an indomitable entrepreneurial spirit, Hill chartered "snow trains" to transport guests from Buffalo, Rochester, and Toronto up to Huntsville and on to Limberlost. He was a true pioneer of winter tourism in Muskoka.

The resort boasted a main lodge with thirteen guest rooms decorated in rustic style, as well as a number of fishing camps with cabins for additional accommodations. Hill had one of the largest stables in all of Muskoka, with more than one hundred horses specifically trained for trail-riding. Sadly, in 1947, Hill died after suffering terrible injuries after a riding accident. His wife, Marion, with the assistance of her daughter and son-in-law, continued to operate the resort for a number of years after his passing.

Limberlost was sold in 1969, and for a time there was a very real threat of modern condominiums being constructed in this untouched wilderness, thereby destroying all that Gordon Hill had built. Thankfully, the concept never developed past the planning stage, and today the former resort operates as Limberlost Forest and Wildlife Reserve, remaining true to Hill's original vision of a place where people can get close to nature.

MAPLEHURST

In its heyday during the Victorian era, Maplehurst was one of the larger resorts on Lake Rosseau, accommodating 125 guests in luxury.

The land upon which Maplehurst was built was sold to English immigrant Joseph Percy Brown by Benjamin Beley (of Rossmoyne Inn fame) in the 1880s. It has been suggested that Brown got himself into some trouble back home that scandalized his family, who sent him into what amounted to exile in the colonies. Whatever the truth of the matter, shortly after arriving, Brown opened his resort. It was the summer of 1886, and the *Toronto Daily Star* at the time noted that Maplehurst was "first class in all its appointments, [and] now open and ready for guests."

Maplehurst, noted for its fine views of the lake and refined atmosphere, was soon doing good business, and Brown did well for himself by marrying into a prominent local family. He was well on his way to making a name for himself. But for reasons that no one has ever been able to surmise, in May of 1897, J.P. Brown committed suicide, ending a life that was short and troubled. Amy Brown persevered despite the loss of her husband, and continued to operate the hotel, with notable success, for more than half a century.

While other resorts began to surpass it in elegance by the early 1900s, Maplehurst retained a fine reputation and it was almost always fully booked.

Maplehurst endured for more than fifty years and was beloved by guests, but it had a troubled history, marred by the suicide of its builder and by a devastating fire that destroyed the elegant building in 1915.

The resort fell victim to a blaze during the winter of 1915 that destroyed the main lodge, leaving only a number of cabins intact. Despite another setback, Mrs. Brown carried on. She converted the dance hall into a new lodge with a kitchen and dining room, and reopened in June of 1916. Unfortunately, the resort's popularity and reputation for elegance could not so easy be replaced, and most of the wealthier guests chose to go to other, more refined resorts.

Amy Brown continued to operate Maplehurst until 1946, when the eighty-four-year-old retired and closed her cherished hotel. While the main building's life came to an abrupt and dramatic end, the Maplehurst that carried on after 1915 ended its proud tradition with a sad whimper: its contents were eventually sold at auction and the building was quietly torn down.

THE MINNEWASKA HOTEL

The Minnewaska Hotel had arguably the most varied history of any resort in Muskoka; while the resort itself was relatively short-lived, the luxurious buildings found new life serving in other roles.

Built in 1897 on the shores of Lake Muskoka, on the outskirts of Gravenhurst, Minnewaska was designed to cater to the well-to-do from Toronto. It seemed well-placed to succeed: it was conveniently located near the railway line linking Muskoka to the city; the majestic brick buildings were outfitted with the most modern of amenities and fine decor; the grounds were expansive and included a fine beach; and there were many recreational opportunities in the form of tennis courts, lawn-bowling pitches, and a billiards room. And yet, the Minnewaska endured for only twenty years before it ceased operations in 1918. Closing the doors was a bitter pill for the owners to swallow, but there were no longer enough guests for it to be profitable. When a generous offer for the property came along, they jumped at it.

The new owners turned the former resort into a hospice for tuberculosis patients called the Calydor Sanatorium. It was believed that fresh country air would cure those stricken, but most remained here for years on end waiting for their symptoms to be relieved. Sadly, many perished at the Calydor. Unlike the neighbouring Muskoka Sanatorium, which accepted people from all walks of life, rich and poor, the Calydor was private and, as befit its luxurious accommodations, accepted only wealthy patients.

During the Second World War, the one-time resort was reinvented once again, and was used to hold prisoners of war. Renamed Camp

214

20, it held up to five hundred men between July 1940 and June 1946 — mostly officers, who made good use of the property's recreational facilities. Often, they would swim and lounge on the very beach that wealthy socialites had enjoyed a half-century earlier.

There were several escape attempts, but only one was successful. A young Luftwaffe pilot, Walter Manhard, disappeared while swimming and was presumed drowned, but in 1991 he reappeared in Gravenhurst on a POW reunion tour. He had escaped to New York, married, and become an American citizen.

Shortly after the war ended, the buildings that had once been the Minnewaska were demolished.

WIGWASSAN LODGE

Around 1900, Frank S. Hurlbut of Toronto built a summer resort on Birch Point, on Tobin Island, located on Lake Rosseau, in the hopes of cashing in on Muskoka's popularity as a tourist destination. He named the property Hotel Waskada, and it enjoyed modest success for a number of years. One element vital to the prosperity of any Muskoka resort proved elusive, however: regular steamer service. Hurlbut just couldn't convince the Muskoka Navigation Company to make his resort a routine stop, as it had done for other properties. After years of trying and repeatedly failing, he bowed out in 1913.

Taking over where Hurlbut left off, an Englishman named Rice tried to make a go of the hotel, but with no more success. The hotel then sat vacant for a number of years. It might have rotted away had it not been for a group of ministers associated with the New York–based chautauqua movement. These ministers were looking for a location in Muskoka where they could establish a summer retreat based upon the principles of religion, education, and exposure to the arts, so when they discovered the empty and available Hotel Waskada, they jumped at the opportunity. Under the ownership of the Canadian Chautauqua Institution Limited, the name of the resort was changed to Epworth Inn, and it became a retreat that focused its programming on religion, literature, music, the arts, and history.

Unfortunately, the resort struggled financially, forcing the Canadian Chautauqua Institution to sell shares in order to finance their idealistic project. One of the new shareholders was George A. Martin. With Epworth Inn floundering, Martin bought the resort and its $15,000 debt outright in 1931. He promptly changed the name to Wigwassan Lodge, a native word meaning "silver birches," and moulded it into a traditional resort. Operating on a shoestring budget and facing the tough times of the Depression, he overcame odds that most would have thought insurmountable. By the end of the decade, he had established Wigwassan as one of the better resorts in the area.

One aspect that set Wigwassan apart from resorts of the day was that staff were not only permitted to mingle with guests, but actually encouraged to do so. This reflected the way the resort was marketed; instead of focusing either on families or well-heeled guests, Martin targeted young, fun-loving, energetic adults. As a result, Wigwassan became one of the liveliest resorts in Muskoka.

In 1963, Martin suffered a coronary and was forced to retire. The new owner, Martin Schill, squandered away what Martin had painstakingly built over three decades — in only three years. Fittingly, both Wigwassan Lodge and George Martin met their ends in 1966.

ACKNOWLEDGEMENTS

The assistance of countless people helped the vision we had for this book become a reality. Some went above and beyond, however, and deserve special mention. Windermere House, Deerhurst Resort, and The Rosseau Resort generously offered comfortable accommodations during our research trips to Muskoka, and their respective staffs were always hospitable, helpful, and forthcoming with their memories. These resorts carry on the finest tradition of Muskoka resorts, and we are indebted to them for the manner in which they embraced this project.

Bruce MacLellan, past-president of the Lake of Bays Heritage Foundation and author of two excellent resources on the history of this oft-overlooked Muskoka lake (*Postcards from Lake of Bays*, *Back Again at Lake of Bays*), kindly offered postcards from his personal collection to illustrate the history of Pulford House and the Alvira Hotel. Similarly, Ian Turnbull and Ron Sclater generously offered the use of postcards from their extensive collections to help illustrate this book. For their part, Kelly Collard and Mary Beley of the Rosseau Historical Society proved invaluable in locating historic photos of Monteith House and the Rossmoyne Inn and pointing us in the right direction for researching these former resorts.

Muskoka's museums are time capsules into its rich and varied past, and we encourage readers to explore them and gain a deeper appreciation for this fascinating region. While the vivid exhibits are what most people see, behind the scenes the curators and their staffs gather and preserve all manner of historical documentation that otherwise would be lost. We've found these museums, in particular Port Carling's Muskoka Lakes Museum and the Muskoka Boat and Heritage Centre in Gravenhurst, to be particularly helpful in researching this book.

We'd like to thank Ken Fowler, formerly the owner of Paignton House and later the Rosseau Resort and Spa, who took the time to reflect on the evolution of the resort industry over the past thirty years, and to write the foreword for this book. We are similarly grateful to Bill Waterhouse, the last of the Waterhouse line to own and operate Deerhurst Resort, who regaled us with tales of his life and the resort in which he grew up.

Finally, we must take the time to thank Barry Penhale and Jane Gibson at Natural Heritage Books/Dundurn Press, whose confidence in this book and in us as authors helped make *Muskoka Resorts: Then and Now* a reality. They have been supporters of our writing for years and deserve to be recognized for the tireless work they do behind the scenes to make our visions a published reality.

This book is further indebted to the following people, who generously provided their time and their memories: Mary Beley, Doug Bishop, Margaret Borton, Jeff Brown, Tim Bryant, Betty Campbell, Kelly Collard, Jean Dickson, Elizabeth Dobson, Shirley Dobson, Terry Einarson, Graeme Ferguson, Ken Fowler, Pearl French, Gillian Godfrey, Jack Hutton, Douglas Johnston, Bruce MacLellan, Norm Mackay, Douglas Pain, Peggy Pain, Rosemary Reid, Bob and Susan Sieber, Ron Sclater, Karen Shopsowitz, Bob Sutton, Jim Swift, Ian Turnbull, Janet Wallace, Barry Walsh, Kim Ward, Bill Waterhouse, and Diane Webster.

Special recognition also is extended to the following institutions for their support: Bala Bay Inn, Baysville Public Library, Bracebridge Public Library, Deerhurst Resort, Dorset Heritage Museum, Gravenhurst Public Library, Huntsville Public Library, Muskoka Boat and Heritage Centre, Muskoka Heritage Place, Muskoka Lakes Museum, Muskoka Lakes Public Library, Rosseau Historical Society, the Rosseau Resort and Spa (a J.W. Marriot Hotel), Windermere Area Archives, and Windermere House.

NOTES

INTRODUCTION

1. George Munro Grant, ed., *Picturesque Canada Volume 2* (Toronto: Belen Bros., 1882).
2. July 2010 interview with the authors.
3. *Ibid.*
4. "Homesteading in Minett," *Muskoka Magazine* (March/April 2001).
5. "Historic Paignton House Building Burns," *Muskoka Advance* (July 2, 2000).

CHAPTER 1: WAWA HOTEL

1. The Canadian Railway News Company was founded in 1883 as a steamship company operating on the Niagara River. It soon moved into the food business, catering to the boom in rail traffic in Canada. The decision to build the WaWa was an extension of its growing interests in the tourism and service industries. Later, in the 1930s, the Canadian Railway News Company began catering to airlines, as well. In 1961, the company changed its name to CARA and moved into the restaurant industry. Today CARA owns

a number of restaurant chains, including Swiss Chalet, Harvey's, and Kelsey's.

2. Charles Orlando Shaw was one of the prominent figures in early twentieth-century Muskoka. Born November 9, 1859, he was the product of a family that for generations had been engaged in the leather-making business. In 1898, he moved from his native America to Huntsville and founded the Anglo-Canadian Leather Company, which eventually evolved into the largest makers of sole leather in the British Empire. Later, he became involved in operating steamships and was president of the Huntsville and Lake of Bays Navigation Company, which was instrumental in fostering the tourism trade in northern Muskoka. C.O. Shaw died in December 1942.

3. Undated brochure from Muskoka Heritage Place archival collection.

4. Bigwin Inn takes its name from the island on which it was built, an island that at one point belonged to Ojibwe chief Bigwin. When Charles Orlando Shaw decided to built a hotel upon Bigwin Island, he shared no expense in its construction, and there was little doubt that, at its height, Bigwin Inn was one of the finest, most exclusive hotels in North America. It was frequented by Hollywood royalty, such as Clark Gable and Carole Lombard, by actual European nobility, and by fabulously wealthy American business people such as the Rockefellers and the Wrigleys.

   After C.O. Shaw died in 1942, the resort passed through several owners and its fortunes declined. For a while, the once-majestic buildings sat empty, and it seemed as if the Bigwin Inn was destined to rot away and disappear from history. Thankfully, new life in the form of an exclusive golf club and condominiums was breathed into the property.

5. Taylor, Cameron. *Enchanted Summers*. Toronto: Lynx Images, 1997: 146.

6. Another version of the story says that Margaret Bowker raced back in to the hotel in search of her missing mother. Most newspaper reports of the time, including the respected *New York Times*, suggest she died in a vain attempt to save her jewellery, so we opted to go with that version of events.

7. *New York Times* (August 23, 1923).

8. The figure for the number of people who perished in the fire varies from source to source. This is largely because some victims didn't die immediately, but rather later succumbed to their injuries while in hospital, making an exact accounting of the dead difficult. Eleven is the commonly accepted figure. Beyond Emily A. McNally, known victims include Margaret Bowker, the young daughter of the Canadian National Railway's general manager; pantry maid Phyllis Benand; linen maid Helen Barrett; a chambermaid identified only as Mrs. James Alexander; Annie Beigh; Elizabeth Carr; and Elizabeth Kroger.
9. Interview with Graeme Ferguson, May 2009.

CHAPTER 2: MONTEITH HOUSE

1. John Hutton was born in Dundee, Scotland. His daughter, Eleanor, was born in the hotel on September 21, 1872. Shortly after Hutton died, his wife, Agnes, remarried. It's believed that she may have wed Walter B. Ross, who succeeded Hutton as proprietor, but there's no concrete proof to back up such claims.
2. The property of A.P. Cockburn's Muskoka Navigation Company, the steamship *Nipissing* was launched in Gravenhurst in 1871. It was 115 feet long and double-decked, a graceful vessel that would become one of the more popular of those ferrying vacationers to area resorts. On August 3, 1886, the *Nipissing* caught fire as it was anchored for the evening at Summit House. The ship was destroyed, but a replacement, the *Nipissing II*, was launched the following year.

   Prior to his arrival in Muskoka, James Kirkland had spent many years aboard vessels on the Great Lakes, and had been skipper of the steamer *Vanderbilt* on Sturgeon Lake in the Kawarthas.
3. Obituary appearing in *Barrie Northern Advance* (September 4, 1902).
4. John Monteith was just one of a string of owners of the Allandale Hotel, which prospered from its location in a community that was a major railway terminus. The Allandale Hotel was founded in 1864 by Ambrose Hamlin and David Wells, but was sold to Samuel Cullen

in 1872. Cullen ran the hotel until 1874, and was then followed by Patrick Hamlin (1875–76), John Monteith (1877–78), and back to Hamlin again (1879–86). The Scott Act, officially the Canada Temperance Act of 1885, made it more difficult to acquire liquor licences, and many hotels closed soon after, the Allandale Hotel among them.

5. Rosseau House was the first summer resort in Muskoka and was the template for all those to follow. In 1869, William H. Pratt, an American, came to Rosseau and purchased several lots. The following May, he built Rosseau House. Incredibly, the resort was open for business on July 1 that year. A resounding success from the start, Pratt continued to expand and refine the resort on an almost yearly basis. For the thirteen years of its existence, it was the heart of village social life, and hosted numerous concerts, dances, and parties.

6. The exact location of the Monteith Hunt Camp has eluded the authors. While some sources suggest it was located in Cardwell Township, it's equally likely it was located in Monteith Township. Information on the hunting retreat is as elusive as its location.

7. The Monteith farm was located on the south side of the Parry Sound Road (modern-day Highway 141) at McCarthy Street. A large barn was located behind the hotel to house the milking cows and the horses that worked the farm. Most of the fields were retained for grazing sheep or haying, though rich berry patches in the hills behind the resort kept fresh pies filled all summer long.

8. Rosseau Historical Society. *Rosseau: The Early Years*, 36.

9. The five children born to John and Catherine Monteith were Gerald, Howard, May, Violet, and Edward. None played any significant role in Monteith House beyond growing up in its gracious surroundings every summer.

10. Little is known about Harry and Jenny's background in their native Poland, or about the exact circumstances that saw them head for Canada. Jenny's lifelong wish to see the family make something of themselves suggests they had modest roots. What little we do know is that Harry was born in 1890 and Jenny four years later, in 1894, and that they came from Kielce, Poland.

11. All Karen Shopsowitz quotes come from an October 2010 interview with the authors.
12. *My Grandparents Owned a Resort* (1990), produced by Karen Shopsowitz.
13. All quotes attributed to Jim Swift come via a September 2010 interview with the authors.

    The Swift Marina had a long and close relationship with Monteith House. It had originally been opened forty years earlier by the Ditchburn brothers, famed Muskoka boat-builders, and from the very beginning they rented out boats to resort guests. The running of the marina was then taken over by Thomas Johnston, and then the Ashdown family, before Clarence and Margarie Swift took ownership in 1949. It remained in the Swift family until 1994, operated for the final thirty years by Jim Swift, Clarence and Margarie's son.
14. All quotes attributed to Terry Einarson come from a September 2010 interview with the authors.

CHAPTER 3: ROSTREVOR

1. John Dinsmore was married to Margaret Anne Jackson, a woman of minor aristocratic background. An example of her standing in Ireland: Margaret Anne once visited her son, Arthur, in Toronto, but returned to Ireland because she did not receive enough "attention" in Canada.
2. Sarah Jane Sheriff was born in 1840 and died in 1919.
3. Edward (1854–1930) became a lumberman and later joined the Queen's Own Rifles, participating in the Riel Rebellion in western Canada. He later became a skilled woodworker and had a carpentry business in Toronto. Joseph, born in 1846, passed away at age 80 in 1926. James, who was born in 1850, disappears from the Dinsmore saga; no date of death is known. Siblings remaining in Ireland were William (1836–?) and Mary Ann (1841–?). Another brother, also named James, died as a youngster (1843–47).

4. Arthur's market farm was located at Spadina Avenue and Bloor Street, and was purchased for $150.

5. The two sons who died young were Arthur Jackson, who passed away at the age of one, and William Jackson, who died at the age of seven, in 1883. The other Dinsmore children were: Robert Sheriff (1868–1939), Annie (1870–1945), Arthur Joseph (1872–1923), John James (1874–1952), Mabel Margaret (1877–1938), Fred Thomas (1880–1951), and Jessica Grace (1883–1920).

6. In addition to running the resort, the Dinsmore boys built numerous cottages and boathouses around the lakes and played a role in building the Royal Muskoka Hotel. During the winters, when all save Fred spent their time in Toronto, they built homes in the city.

7. All quotes from Gillian Godfrey come from email exchanges during June of 2010.

8. All quotes from Liz Dobson come from an interview with the authors dated October 13, 2010.

9. All quotes from Doug Bishop date to an August 2010 email exchange.

CHAPTER 4: DEERHURST RESORT

1. All quotes from Bill Waterhouse date to a November 2006 interview.

2. Edward Waterhouse accompanied Charles to Canada in 1884. Like Charles, Edward entered the hotel industry, if only briefly, by purchasing the Portage Hotel on Peninsula Lake. He lasted seven years there, then sold the business and sought a new life in the North-West Territories. Things didn't pan out there either, and he eventually returned to Ontario.

3. Charles Waterhouse was a talented thespian and musician. A review of an 1895 theatre production he was involved with ran in the *Huntsville Forester*, and suggested that he "as usual, appeared to be the general favourite and was a whole concert in himself." His penchant for entertaining would later help attract guests back to Deerhurst year after year.

4. Hylda Hartley was born in 1868. She had come to Canada in June 1896 to visit her brother, Roger, another Aspdin settler, and ended up never returning home. She met Charles Waterhouse, fell in love, and a year later was married at St. Anne's Anglican Church in Toronto.

5. Charles Thomas Simcox seems to have been a friend of Charles Waterhouse from London, England, and though he was often referred to in the press of the time as co-proprietor, he was, in fact, a silent partner. He sold his shares back to Charles Waterhouse in 1907 for a mere $1,500, seven hundred dollars less than they were worth, indicating the relationship was based on friendship rather than strictly a business arrangement.

6. *Huntsville Standard* (July 23, 1903).

7. *Huntsville Forester* (July 26, 1906).

8. Kennedy, Laura. *Deerhurst Resort: A Century of Hospitality in North Muskoka*. Erin, On: The Boston Mills Press, 1995: 13–14.

9. *Huntsville Standard* (June 5, 1900).

10. In retirement, Charles continued to live at the resort from time to time, but spent most summers in Algonquin Park and winters either in England or Toronto. He died in London on September 30, 1931. In his absence, Hylda returned to Canada to live with her son and his family. She remained a visible presence at Deerhurst until her death in 1948.

11. Kennedy, Laura. *Deerhurst Resort: A Century of Hospitality in North Muskoka*. Erin, On: The Boston Mills Press: 31.

12. The Britannia Hotel was one of Muskoka's most famous and luxurious resorts. Founder Thomas J. White spotted the beautiful property on which it was located during a canoe trip in 1901, after which he purchased it. He began building the hotel in 1907, and it opened for its first summer a year later. In 1955, White's son Paul began a full-scale transformation of the Britannia. The aging original building was torn down and a modern, all-season building was erected in its place. To truly make the resort into a year-round operation, a curling rink, a ski hill and trails, and conference facilities were added. The buildings still stand today, but the Britannia has long been closed.

13. The idea for Hidden Valley began in 1959, when twenty-six-year-old Bill Waterhouse saw an opportunity to develop a major ski attraction for Muskoka. Huntsville's tourism industry shut down in October and the resorts with it, leaving supporting industries without business until spring. Bill and a friend, Graham Brown, pooled $1,000 to establish a ski club. By 1961, the slopes were open. In 1965, Bill built a new hotel adjacent to the ski hill under the auspices of Holiday Inn. Hidden Valley helped transform Muskoka into an all-season tourist destination.

CHAPTER 5: SHAMROCK LODGE

1. Benjamin Hardcastle Johnston was born at Wynchford Bridge, County Meath, Ireland. He immigrated to Canada around 1850 and originally settled and farmed in Nissouri Township, London, Ontario. A decade later, he uprooted his family and headed for Muskoka, enticed there by the Free Land Grants. Benjamin Hardcastle was one of the first settlers in Port Carling and is considered its founding father. He became the community's first postmaster in 1869, and it was he who named the community, after John Carling, the minister of Public Works and a personal friend. He died at Port Carling on August 7, 1893.

   Benjamin had four sons: Gary, Benjamin Jr., William, and Robert Hardcastle. Little is known of Gary Johnston, including his dates of birth and death, or even where he was buried. He wed, but never had any children, and spent his entire life hunting and fur-trapping in and around Mactier and Foot's Bay, on Lake Joseph. There is even less information on Benjamin. All that is known is that he never married and died a young man. William was born in 1851, and died in 1935. Robert Hardcastle was born in 1852, was married to Ismay James, and died in 1936.

2. Other sources suggest Robert Hardcastle Johnston gained title to the land by paying twenty-five dollars to the government and

offering the white horse to the Ojibwe of the area as a token gesture of goodwill.

3. Wild Goose Lodge was built by Benjamin Johnston in Brackenrig shortly after he arrived in Muskoka, envisioning it as a place where settlers, government land surveyors, and sportsmen could find a warm bed. Over time, it began catering mostly to recreational hunters and fishers. "It was located on property that was for many years occupied by Penny's Saw Mill," remembers Douglas Johnston, a great-grandson of Benjamin through Robert Hardcastle. "Over the years (mill owner) Dudley Penney informed me on different occasions in the process of digging around the property that he uncovered a variety of broken dishes, pots, and pans that at one time served as Benjamin's kitchen". No one knows exactly how long the Wild Goose Lodge was in operation, but it didn't survive Benjamin's move into Port Carling.

4. There were actually two *Shamrocks*. The first operated for a few short years from 1903, until it was sold. The second was purchased in 1907. An attractive vessel built specifically as a yacht, she was twenty-five feet long and weighed in at about ten tons. The *Shamrock II* was eventually sold and became the property of Thomas and Alfred Croucher, who renamed her *Niska* and employed the once-elegant yacht as a scow, towing logs to area sawmills. It remained in service until the 1940s, and was said to be the last tug on Lake Rosseau to tow a boom of logs.

5. Robert Hardcastle Johnston, who stood a powerful five foot ten inches tall, was known to be extremely handy with a broad axe (an axe with a fourteen-inch blade designed for squaring timber). One anecdote, as recorded by grandson Douglas Robert Johnston in a collection of vignettes about his grandparents and verified by older members of the community, suggests something of his ability:

> Following a few libations (at the North Star Hotel in Port Carling), some of the workers would start boasting and squabbling about their expertise in the use of this instrument (the broad axe). Loose tongues would

encourage betting about one's accuracy and expertise with this axe. More drinks flowed and the evening wore on. The challenge was to place a wooden match on the floor, then from shoulder height swing the axe downward with full force to split it lengthwise. We were always given to understand that grandfather collected on more occasions than he had to pay.

Robert Hardcastle Johnston's axe was donated to the Muskoka Lakes Museum in Port Carling and remains on display today.

6. Robert Hardcastle Johnston and his wife, Ismay James, had six children in total: Robert Hugh, William J., Benjamin, Alfred, Sarah, and John Taylor. Robert Hugh was born in 1879 and died in 1967, never having married; William J. was born in 1881, and he wed Mae Sands but they had no children; Benjamin, born in 1882, died at eleven years old, in 1893; Alfred was born in 1885 and married Annie Leslie — they had two girls, Wanda and Jean; Sarah was born in 1890, but she survived only a few short years, dying in 1893; John Taylor, the final Johnston child, was born in 1892. He married Lucie Gibson and together they had two children, Lauretta and Douglas. John died in 1960.

7. Douglas Johnston, July 2010 exchange.

8. Information on Bill and Eve Clinch comes courtesy of Jane Clinch Hannaby of Gravenhurst, a niece of the former owners.

9. All quotes attributed to Tim Bryant come from a June 2007 interview at Shamrock Lodge.

CHAPTER 6: ROSSMOYNE INN

1. Much of the information on Benjamin Beley and the early years at Rossmoyne comes courtesy of Mary Beley of Rosseau, during August 2006 exchanges with the authors.

2. Lucy Beley (née Dawson) was born in Llangan, Wales, on June 8, 1839, and was the daughter of a clergyman. It was the glowing

praise of her brother, who came to Canada to work on a survey of the Nipissing Road, which convinced the young couple to immigrate to Canada; originally, they had considered moving to New Zealand. She died on December 24, 1899.

3. Pauline Johnston, the daughter of a Mohawk chief and an Englishwoman, was one of Canada's most famed poets in the early twentieth century. She spent many summers vacationing in Rosseau, and it was during one of these summers that she paddled up the Shadow River and was so inspired by its beauty that she wrote one of her most popular poems, entitled simply "Shadow River." While the waterway was already popular with vacationers, due in large part to the seemingly magical way in which the waters reflected images of overhanging tree branches, Johnston's poem made the river famous across North America.

4. Fanita "Fanny" Turner was remarkably close to the Beleys. She sometimes acted as a companion to their eldest daughter, Mary Eliza; their youngest daughter was named after her; and, according to Benjamin's diaries, she acted as his secretary one summer when he took ill.

5. All quotes attributed to Margaret Borton are sourced to an April 2009 interview with the authors.

6. The children of Benjamin and Lucy included: Charles Kingsbury, born March 7, 1868, died November 1949 in Rosseau; John William, born October 15, 1869, died January 25, 1938 in Calgary; Mary Eliza (Birdie), born October 5, 1871, died March 8, 1951 (married Dr. Richard Ussher Topp); George Alfred, born May 9, 1873, died May 24, 1947; James Maclennan, born December 25, 1876, died December 13, 1927, in Memphis, Tennessee; Elizabeth Mabel Edith, born November 17, 1878, died December 29, 1878; Ethel May, born August 18, 1881, died December 22, 1964 [married John Sirett Lloyd Dawson (July 30, 1880–July 6, 1930)]; Fanita Isabelle, born December 17, 1885, died June 7, 1975 (married Alexander Fraser).

7. Joseph Ariss immigrated to Canada with his parents and his brother William in 1877. He came to Muskoka in 1878 and was employed by Benjamin Beley on his farm for $14 a month. He died in 1956. Emma had predeceased him, passing away in 1951. Their

son Harold was born in 1890 and wed Jean Boyd, who was born in Scotland in 1900 and was one of ten children (known siblings include sisters Net, Minnie, Charlotte, and Elizabeth, and brothers Andrew, Jim, and Charlie).

8. Memoirs of Dianne Webster, provided October 2010.

9. Interview with Margaret Borton conducted by the authors in March 2009.

10. Memoirs of Dianne Webster, provided October 2010.

11. All quotes credited for Pearl French came during a March 2009 interview with the authors.

12. Interview with Diane Webster conducted by the authors in April 2009.

CHAPTER 7: PROSPECT HOUSE

1. Little is known of Sarah Cox's life before her marriage to Enoch in 1847.

2. The boarding house was located near the Royal Opera House, the only opera house in Toronto, and in the centre of the city's entertainment district. As a result, many theatrical people roomed there. "They were very good company," remembered Seymour Penson, "and helped to make Cox's a more interesting and cheerful place than the average boarding house."

3. Penson, 170.

4. The Cox children were as follows: Fanny (married Edwin Potts, a Toronto picture framer); Polly (wed Alfred Burges, a plumber); Sally (married a clerk named Dick Rowe); Edith (wife of Captain John Rogers); and George "Edward."

5. Penson, 170. John Rogers was something of an adventurer and an important figure in early Muskoka. Born February 14, 1846, in Derbyshire, England, as a young man he studied law and engineering, worked on a railroad, built diving machines, served aboard a merchant ship, and operated seawater distillers in Arabia. He produced stunningly accurate maps for the *Guide and Atlas to Muskoka*

and Parry Sound District 1879, and never left, operating steamships on the Muskoka Lakes until his death on May 31, 1926.

6. John and Elizabeth Jones had settled in Muskoka in 1880, living near Prospect House, where John worked as a porter. They moved to the Port Carling area in 1895, and opened Pinelands in 1906. The resort, known for its spartan simplicity, also became the post office for this section of the lake. In 1942, John and Elizabeth's sons, Clarence and Albert, added the adjacent Belmont House to Pinelands and operated them jointly as Pinelands Lodges. By the 1970s, the original Pinelands was in such a state of decay that it had to be torn down.

7. As remembered by great-granddaughter Rosemary Reid in a June 2009 interview.

8. The position of Port Sandfield's postmaster was something of a Cox family tradition: Enoch served as the village's first postmaster from 1882 to 1898, and was succeeded upon his death by his son, Edward, who served until 1933; Marianne Rogers, the daughter of Captain John Rogers and Enoch Cox's granddaughter, held the position until 1945; finally, her brother, Enoch Rogers, handled the mail until 1949, at which time the position passed out of the family after sixty-seven years.

CHAPTER 8: PULFORD HOUSE

1. William H. Brown, widely hailed today as Baysville's founder, was an important local businessman who operated mills and ran the post office from his home. Brown (January 22, 1840–December 29, 1920) wed Elizabeth Henderson (January 25, 1833–June 16, 1909) on March 10, 1863.

2. Emmeline died around the time Pulford would have been born, quite likely from complications during childbirth (she would have been fifty-three years old at the time). It seems likely, therefore, that Pulford Henderson was named to honour his deceased mother.

3. J.J.'s father, George Robertson, an engineer, originally hailed from Scotland. He was born in 1847 and came to Canada in 1872. After a

brief stop in Montreal, he made for Muskoka and the free land grants being offered there. He settled on Norway Point in 1873. Two years later he met and married Elizabeth Forest (1852–1873), a nurse. A year later, J.J was born. His birth was a big deal at the time: Chief Bigwin and his tribe came across Lake of Bays from their home on Bigwin Island to see the infant — the first white baby born in the area — and brought with them several large fish as a generous gift to celebrate the occasion. Other children born to George and Elizabeth Robertson were Katherine (Lush), Janet (Laing), and Margaret (Thompson).

George Robertson died in 1903, after which time J.J. took over the Norway Point homestead. He sold the land to the Canadian Railway News Company, which erected the WaWa Hotel there in 1908. In selling the land to the CRNC, Robertson inadvertently introduced his three sisters to their respective husbands: Katherine married Howard Lush, an electrician employed onsite during construction; Janet married Edgar Laing, who was working his way through dental college by playing in the hotel band; and Margaret married the hotel manager, Allan Thompson.

J.J. Robertson had his own connection to the WaWa: during the off-season he served as the property caretaker. For more information on the WaWa Hotel, see Chapter 1.

4. All quotes from Jean Dickson were from an October 2004 interview.

5. Elizabeth "Libbie" Beatrice Robertson (née Langford), a Baysville schoolteacher, outlived her husband by several decades, dying in October 1968. She was the daughter of Mark and Elizabeth Langford, early Baysville settlers.

6. All quotes attributed to Betty Campbell were from an interview conducted in May 2004.

7. All quotes attributed to Barry Walsh come from an interview conducted in April 2010.

8. Because the main lodge was gone, every available space was given over to guestrooms. In addition to the three cabins, guests could stay in one of several rooms attached to the dance hall, within the refurbished boathouse, or even in the Walsh's own home, the former staff quarters.

CHAPTER 9: ALVIRA HOTEL

1. For the first decades of Dorset's existence, before the arrival of steamships on Lake of Bays in the 1890s, the Bobcaygeon Colonization Road (also known as the Snowden Road) was the community's sole link to the outside world. Part of a network of roads designed in the mid-nineteenth century to open up areas in central and eastern Ontario for settlement and development, the Bobcaygeon Colonization Road ran from Bobcaygeon in the south, through Minden, and on to Dorset in the north.

2. George Edward Langford (1859–1941) was a prominent figure in Muskoka. A one-time reeve of Bracebridge, he rose to become Muskoka's representative in the Legislative Assembly of Ontario from 1894–98 as a Conservative.

3. The village of Dorset got its start in 1859 when the Bobcaygeon Road reached Lake of Bays. Tavern-keeper Zac Cole is widely recognized as being the founder of the community, and for a while the community was named Colebridge. When he applied for a post office in 1883 he found that a Colebridge already existed. The name Dorset was chosen instead, probably because the surveyor, Thomas Ridout, came from Dorset, England.

   In 1874, James B. Shrigley established a sawmill and gristmill at what was then little more than a handful of rude cabins, giving the community a welcome boost. More important was the arrival of lumbermen a few years later. Lumber companies commenced extensive logging operations around the Hollow River watershed, particularly around Lake Kawagama and into Algonquin Park. Shrigley's mill was too small and the community too isolated for the thousands of logs harvested each year to be cut locally. Instead, the logs were guided across Lake of Bays and down the South Muskoka River to Bracebridge, where larger mills and access to rail lines ensured greater profits. For almost three decades, Dorset was the heart of these lucrative timber-harvesting operations.

3. The Iroquois Hotel was located across the street from the Alvira Hotel, with whom it competed for guests and prestige. It began in the 1880s as

Dorset House, an unpretentious little boarding house catering to traffic straggling along the Old Bobcaygeon Road, but eventually grew into the largest hotel in Dorset under the name the Iroquois Hotel. At various times it was known as the McIlroy Hotel, the Narrows Hotel, and the Lumberjack Inn. Today, it is the home of the Fiery Grill Restaurant.

4. Notes from Dorset Heritage Museum.

5. Captain George F. Marsh was instrumental in the development of Lake of Bays. He first lived in Baysville, where he dabbled in lumbering and farming, then moved to the mouth of the Oxtongue River, where he operated a sawmill and, in 1878, built his first steamship, the *Mary Louise*. Other vessels would soon follow, so that by the time he formed the Huntsville and Lake of Bays Transportation Company in 1895, he had ten steamships and enjoyed a monopoly on the lake. He was also responsible for building the Portage Railway, linking Peninsula Lake to Lake of Bays, famed for being the shortest railway system in the world at one mile in length. When Marsh died in 1904, he could rest easy knowing that he had succeeded in driving off all competitors and created a thriving business. The new owner, C.O. Shaw, would rename the business The Huntsville and Lake of Bays Navigation Company and take it to even greater heights.

6. Interview with Norm MacKay, May 2008.

7. Isaac Newton and Eunice Alvira Langford had three children, all of them born in Dorset: Roy Seburn (born October 4, 1895); Angus Melville (born December 20, 1898); and Louis Newton Hobart (born November 21, 1899).

CHAPTER 10: ELGIN HOUSE

1. The Love family is of Irish descent, but immigrated to Canada in 1803. They established a homestead along Yonge Street, in the wilderness north of Toronto, which later developed into a thriving farm. A small hamlet rose up in the vicinity and, taking the name of the first settlers, became known as Love's Corners (now part of Richmond Hill).

Lambert Love was one of nine children born to Robert Love and Mary Ann Fleury, a young woman whose family owned the Fleury Iron Works, one of the largest manufacturers of farming machinery in Canada at the time.

2. Some writers have suggested that the sawmill did poor business, and that it was a dismal failure for Love. That's far from accurate, as it seemed never to be short of work. "The sawmill buzzed day in and day out, belching smoke and steam but turning out very sweet smelling lumber of pine, ash, oak, and hemlock. The aroma still lingers in my subconscious mind to this day," wrote Lambert Elgin in an article published posthumously in the *Muskoka Sun* (September 1, 1988). Simply put, while the mill was busy and profitable, operating it didn't provide for Love in the manner in which he desired.

3. "Elgin House from Its Start Through the Years," *The Muskoka Sun* (September 1, 1988).

4. *Ibid.*

5. "Commentary and Corrections.... Concerning 'Muskoka's Grand Hotels,'" *Muskoka Sun* (August 25, 1988).

6. Dates for lighting and generator additions. In 1920, Lambert Love invested in the new Bala Electric Light and Power Company, which brought electric lights to Port Carling and the environs, possibly with the hope that one day it would bring hydro to Elgin House.

7. Glen Home was located across the lake from Elgin House, near the village of Glen Orchard. It opened on July 29, 1939, at which point Lambert was eighty-four years old. Glen Home's founder died eight years later, but the resort carried on under Lambert's second wife, Alice, and his son, Paul, for many successful decades. It finally closed in 1974, one year after Alice passed away. The property was purchased by the Sisters of St. Joseph, a Roman Catholic order. Members renamed it Mary Grove and used it as a retreat. Sadly, the building was torn down in 2008.

8. "Elgin House from Its Start Through the Years," *The Muskoka Sun* (September 1, 1988).

9. "Friends Thank Elgin House for Memories Since 1928," *The Muskoka Sun* (August 29, 1991).

10. *Ibid.*

11. Being a hotelier was in Michael Grice's blood, and three of his siblings likewise operated summer resorts: John and Peter operated Delawana Inn, while Fred ran Aston Resort.

12. All quotes attributed to Cathy Tait are from an October 2007 interview.

CHAPTER 11: PAIGNTON HOUSE

1. The Wrenshall brothers were two of the earliest settlers on the peninsula, arriving in Canada in 1865, and Muskoka a year later. They settled on the point where the famous Royal Muskoka Hotel would later be built, but experienced little real success, despite their innovative approach to obtaining free labour.

2. Thorel House was built in 1914 by George R. Thorel. George Thorel was a relative newcomer, only arriving in the region in 1894. Thorel House embraced dancing and lively music, even while most resorts in the area shunned such interruptions to their sedate, tranquil atmospheres. Thorel House was also very modern, boasting electric lighting, running water in every room, and a bathroom on each floor. The resort stood until demolished in 1968.

3. "Homesteading in Minett," *Muskoka Magazine* (March/April 2001).

4. Michael Woods was born in Liverpool, England, in 1848, and immigrated to Canada as a young man. He first settled in Toronto, where he was a warden at the jail. When he received a death threat from an inmate, he decided it was time to relocate. He moved to Muskoka in 1882. In 1894, he built Woodington Resort, a large and prosperous hotel that, by 1916, could accommodate as many as 125 guests. Michael Woods died in 1927. The resort remained in the family with his daughter, Nancy May Anderson, until 1965. It trudged on under new owners until 1973.

5. All quotes credited to Doug Pain are from an October 2010 interview with the authors.

6. "Homesteading in Minett," *Muskoka Magazine* (March/April 2001).

7. *Ibid.*
8. *Ibid.* The Royal Muskoka Hotel was almost certainly the most prestigious resort in Muskoka, at least until the Bigwin Inn arrived on the scene in 1920. The Royal Muskoka opened in 1901, setting a new standard for accommodation in Muskoka. Whereas most area resorts were owned by a single individual or family, the Royal was developed by the Muskoka Lakes Navigation and Hotel Company, with the Grand Trunk Railway as a partner. Every conceivable comfort was available here, including hairdressers, a barber, newsstands, a bakery, and a long-distance telephone exchange. The resort fell on hard times during the Depression and burned to the ground in 1952.
9. "Homesteading in Minett," *Muskoka Magazine* (March/April 2001).
10. Betty came from a family that was as involved in the development of Muskoka as the Pains. The Copes had long operated Ferndale Resort, while her mother was a Sutton, a family that played a prominent part in early Port Carling (E.B. Sutton built the Swastika Hotel, today known as the Bala Bay Inn). Betty's parents were business people in their own right, running a butcher shop and ice cream parlour in Port Carling.
11. All quotes from Janet Wallace come from a November 2010 interview with the authors.
12. All quotes from Ken Foster come from a November 2010 interview with the authors.
13. "Century-Old Resort Damaged by Fire," *The Muskokan* (July 6, 2000).
14. "Childhood Memories at One of Muskoka's Great Resorts." *The Muskokan* (September 18, 2008).

CHAPTER 12: WINDERMERE HOUSE

1. There is some debate about when Thomas Aitken arrived at Windermere. Seymour Penson, a contemporary who made note of new arrivals around Lake Rosseau in his journals, suggests he came

to Muskoka in 1860. Family members tell us he stopped in Otonabee Township (Peterborough County) for a number of years, and that it was 1863 when he arrived. They also suggest he left Windermere for a while to work on steamers on the Great Lakes. Penson is probably correct; his journals have proven remarkably accurate. There may be some truth in family lore, however. Until their farms were well-established, many settlers spent only part of their year in Muskoka, returning to civilization for the balance. It's therefore possible that Aitken arrived in Muskoka in 1860, spent parts of the next few years as a Great Lakes sailor, and only began to live full time in Muskoka in 1863.

2. It was Thomas Aitken who convinced David Fife, his brother-in-law, to move to Canada. He came in 1863, cleared some land in Windermere, and moved his family there in 1868. In 1889, his son, David Fife Jr., built a resort of his own to the east of Windermere House, just across the road. Fife House, as the summer hotel was called, was a popular destination in its own right. After briefly passing out of family hands, Arthur Fife took ownership of the property and continued its operation until his death in 1960. In many ways Fife House and Windermere House enjoyed a shared identity, so it made sense when Mary Elizabeth Aitken purchased the hotel and joined it with Windermere House. Fife House was later torn down and replaced by the exclusive Windermere Cottages fractional units.

3. The Eaton and Aitken families became extremely close over the years. Minnie Aitken, Thomas's daughter, was a close friend since childhood to Sir John Eaton, Timothy Eaton's son. Minnie later wed and moved to Winnipeg, which naturally put distance between them, but when Minnie became deathly ill in 1920, Sir John sent his private rail car to bring her back to Windermere for her final days. The Eatons had a summer home, Kawandag, near Rosseau.

4. Susan Pryke, *Windermere House: The Tradition Continues* (Erin, ON: Boston Mills Press, 1999), 23.

5. *Ibid.*, 25.

6. *Ibid.*, 27.

7. *Ibid.*

8. Interview with the authors, May 2010.

BIBLIOGRAPHY

Armstrong, Martha. "Century-Old Resort Damaged by Fire," *The Muskokan*. July 6, 2000.

Boyer, Barbaranne. *Muskoka's Grand Hotels*. Erin, ON: The Boston Mills Press, 1987.

Canadian Summer Resorts: Illustrated Souvenir and Guide. Toronto: F. Smily, 1900.

Chenhall, Mary. "Friends Thank Elgin House for Memories Since 1928," *The Muskokan*. 1991.

Coate, Dorothy. *Coate Family Archive*. Bracebridge Public Library.

Coombe, Geraldine. *Muskoka Past and Present*. Toronto: McGraw-Hill Ryerson, 1976.

Cope, Leila M. *A History of the Village of Port Carling*. Bracebidge, ON: Herald-Gazette Press, 1956.

Cumberland, Barlow. *Muskoka and the Northern Lakes*. 1886.

Denison, John. *Micklethwaite's Muskoka*. Erin, ON: The Boston Mills Press, 1993.

DuVernet, Sylvia. "The Dinsmores: Family Who Created Rostrevor," *Muskoka Sun*.

Fife, Matthew James. *Down Memory Lane*. Self-published.

Findlay, Mary Lynn. *Lures and Legends of Lake of Bays*. Bracebridge, ON: 1973.

Grant, George Munro, ed. *Picturesque Canada Volume 2*. Toronto: Belen Bros., 1882.

Hamilton, W.E., ed. *Guide Book and Atlas of Muskoka and Parry Sound Districts*. Toronto: H.R. Page, 1879.

Hosking, Carol. *Clevelands House — Summer Memories*. Erin, ON: The Boston Mills Press, 1993.

Hutton, Jack. "Bala Bay Inn Gets a New Lease on Life," *Muskoka Sun*. June 29, 2006.

_____. "Bala Bay Inn Has Links to Poet Robert Browning," *Muskoka Sun*. July 15, 2010.

Jocque, Violet. *Pioneers and Latecomers*. Minett, ON: 1979.

Kennedy, Laura. *Deerhurst Resort — A Century of Hospitality in Northern Muskoka*. Erin: The Boston Mills Press, 1995.

Levey, Barbara. "Rules Were Strict in the House Love Built," *The Muskokan*. October 4, 2001.

Lockhart, Sandy. "Homesteading in Minett," *Muskoka Magazine*. March/April 2001.

Love, Lambert. "Elgin House from Its Start Through the Years: Reminiscences of the Late Lambert Love Jr.," *Muskoka Sun*. September 1, 1988.

Love, Lisa and Paul. "Commentary and Corrections ... Concerning 'Muskoka's Grand Hotels,'" *Muskoka Sun*. August 25, 1988.

MacLellan, Bruce. *Postcards from Lake of Bays*. Self-published, 2007.

_____. *Back Again at Lake of Bays*. Self-published, 2010.

McTaggart, Douglas. *Bigwin Inn*. Erin, ON: The Boston Mills Press, 1992.

Muskoka Lakes Association. *Summertimes: In Celebration of 100 Years of the Muskoka Lakes Association*. Erin, ON: The Boston Mills Press, 1994.

"Old Muskoka Resorts: Bala Bay Inn," *The Muskokan*. September 3, 1987.

Patchet, Pamela. "Childhood Memories at One of Muskoka's Great Resorts," *The Muskokan*. September 18, 2008.

Peninsula Lake Association Historical Committee. *Pen Lake: Reflections of Peninsula Lake*. Erin, Ontario: The Boston Mills Press, 1994.

Penson, Seymour. "Seymour Penson and His Muskoka Neighbours, Part II," *East Georgian Bay Historical Journal Volume IV*. Meaford, ON: East Georgian Bay Historical Foundation, 1985.

Pryke, Susan. *Explore Muskoka*. Erin, ON: The Boston Mills Press, 1987.

_____. *Explore Muskoka Lakes*. Erin, ON: The Boston Mills Press, 1990.

_____. *The History of Clevelands House: Magic Summers*. Erin, ON: The Boston Mills Press, 2001.

_____. *Windermere House: The Tradition Continues*. Toronto: The Boston Mills Press, 1999.

Research Committee of the Muskoka Pioneer Village. *Huntsville: Pictures from the Past*. Erin, Ontario: The Boston Mills Press, 1986.

Rice, Harmon E. *Brief Centennial History of Huntsville*. Huntsville, ON: Forester Press, 1964.

Rogers, John. *Muskoka Lakes Blue Book, Directory and Chart*. Toronto: 1915.

Roper, Edward. *Muskoka: The Picturesque Playground of Canada*. Toronto: Hart and Company, 1915.

Rosseau Historical Society. *Rosseau: The Early Years*. Rosseau, ON: 1999.

_____. *Rosseau: Then and Now*. Rosseau, ON: 2004.

Summertimes: In Celebration of 100 Years of the Muskoka Lakes Association. Erin, ON: The Boston Mills Press, 1994.

Sutton, Frederick William. *Early History of Bala*. Bracebridge, ON: Herald-Gazette Press, 1970.

Tatley, Richard. *The Steamboat Era in the Muskokas: Volume 1 — To the Golden Years*. Erin: The Boston Mills Press, 1983.

_____. *The Steamboat Era in the Muskokas: Volume II — The Golden Years to the Present*. Erin: The Boston Mills Press, 1983.

Taylor, Cameron. *Enchanted Summers*. Toronto: Lynx Images, 1997.

Turnbull, Scott. "The Story of Wigwassan Lodge," *Muskoka Sun*. June 10, 1999.

Vardon, Roger (a.k.a Frederick DelaFosse). *English Bloods*. Graphic Publishers Limited, 1930.

Young, Scott. "Historic Paignton House Building Burns," *Muskoka Advance*. July 2, 2000.

MANUSCRIPTS AND DIARIES

An Aitken Family Lineage, Mona Aitken
Baysville Area Women's Institute, Tweedsmuir History
Diary of Benjamin S. Beley
Fife Family Papers
Memoirs of Dianne Webster
Minute Books of the Village of Rosseau
Peninsula Women's Institute, Tweedsmuir History
S.R.G. Penson Memoirs
Windermere Women's Institute, Tweedsmuir History

ADDITIONAL NEWSPAPERS REFERENCED

Barrie Northern Advance
Bracebridge Examiner
Bracebridge Herald-Gazette
Gravenhurst News
Huntsville Forester
Huntsville Standard
Muskoka Advance
Muskoka Sun
The Muskokan
New York Times
Northern Advocate
Orillia Packet
Toronto World

FILM

My Grandparents Had a Hotel, produced by Karen Shopsowitz

INDEX

....

ABOUT THE AUTHORS

Andrew Hind and Maria Da Silva are freelance writers who live in Bradford, Ontario. They specialize in history and travel, particularly in Muskoka, a region they've come to intimately know and love. Both cottage in the region and have spent years exploring while writing for a number of local publications. They contribute regular features to *Muskoka Magazine*, and their work can also be seen in the pages of other regional newspapers and magazines, such as *The Muskokan*, *Muskoka*

Life, Muskoka Sideroads, and *Beyond the City.* Beyond Muskoka, Andrew and Maria's articles have appeared in a host of national and international publications, among them the *Toronto Star, Horizons, Lakeland Boating,* the *Globe and Mail,* and *Paranormal.*

Muskoka: Then and Now represents Andrew and Maria's ninth book. Previous publications include *Ghost Towns of Muskoka* (Dundurn Press, 2008), which examines the tragic history of a collection of communities from across Muskoka whose stars have long since faded, and *Ghosts of Niagara-on-the-Lake* (Dundurn Press, 2009), in which the haunted heritage of this charming and historic community is explored. Some of their other titles include *Niagara: Daredevils, Danger, and Unforgettable Stories* (Folklore Publishing, 2009), *Secrets of Lake Simcoe* (James Lorimer, 2010), and *Cottage Country Ghosts* (Ghost House Books, 2010).

Together, Andrew and Maria host historical and paranormal guided tours, which aim to bring history alive in an intimate, tangible fashion. They can be reached at *maelstrom@symopatico.ca* or *dasilvababy@hotmail.com.*

ALSO BY ANDREW HIND
AND MARIA DA SILVA

Ghosts of Niagara-on-the-Lake
978-1-55488-387-5 $24.99

Long-dead soldiers, grieving lovers, the heroic
Laura Secord — Niagara-on-the-Lake's long
and colourful history is kept alive by the ghosts
of its past. Widely considered Canada's most
haunted community, the town has preserved
many of its historical buildings — perfect
haunts for age-old spirits. Come and explore
one of Canada's most fascinating towns.

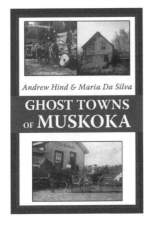

Ghost Towns of Muskoka
978-1-55002-796-9 $24.99

Explore the tragic history of a collection
of communities across Muskoka, and get
to know the people who lived, loved, and
laboured in these small wilderness settlements.
This book brings to life the stories of a time
when the forests of Muskoka were flooded
with loggers and land-hungry settlers.

Available at your favourite bookseller.

www.dundurn.com

What did you think of this book?
Visit *www.duundurn.com* for reviews, videos, updates, and more!

Marquis Book Printing Inc.

Québec, Canada
2011